An Introduction to Educational Law

An Introduction to Educational Law

For Administrators and Teachers

By

Joseph J. Cobb, Ph.D.

Associate Professor
College of Education
Wright State University
Dayton, Ohio

CHARLES C THOMAS • PUBLISHER
Springfield • Illinois • U.S.A.

Published and Distributed Throughout the World by
CHARLES C THOMAS • PUBLISHER
Bannerstone House
301-327 East Lawrence Avenue, Springfield, Illinois, U.S.A.

© *1981, by* CHARLES C THOMAS • PUBLISHER
ISBN 0-398-04158-X
Library of Congress Catalog Card Number: 80-23395

*With THOMAS BOOKS careful attention is given to all details of
manufacturing and design. It is the Publisher's desire to present books that are
satisfactory as to their physical qualities and artistic possibilities and appropriate
for their particular use. THOMAS BOOKS will be true to those laws of quality
that assure a good name and good will.*

Cobb, Joseph J
    An introduction to educational law for administrators and teachers.

    Bibliography: p.
    Includes indexes.
    1. Educational law and legislation—United States.
I. Title.
KF4119.C6   344.73′07   80-23395
ISBN 0-398-04158-X

Printed in the United States of America
PS-RX-1

To Kathy and Runt
Two people who help turn
dreams into realities

PREFACE

This book is an introduction to Educational Law. It deals primarily with laws relating to the operations of public schools (both elementary and secondary).

This book is designed not only for students in the field of education but also for others concerned with the implications of school law, and the material is such that any interested layman and educator can readily grasp the content.

School law is not static, nor should it be viewed as a separate branch of law. Recent years have witnessed a proliferation in the magnitude of school-related statutory enactments, federal legislation, and court decisions. These legal enactments and interpretations are having a far-ranging impact on the lives of all who are associated with education—children, parents, teachers, administrators, as well as boards of education.

It is essential that those who must operate within the education arena understand the basic principles of educational law. This is of utmost importance if one is to be effective in the operation of schools. It is the purpose of this publication to supply the basic understanding in nontechnical language to educators and others without legal training.

Except for Chapter 1, which is intended for those unfamiliar with the origin and operation of the law, each chapter focuses on the legal aspects of a problem area in education. Within each chapter, fundamental concepts are introduced and form recurring themes. The book is designed as a teaching-learning vehicle; for this reason, it is dedicated to a panoramic view of the complex field rather than an in-depth analysis of each major dimension of law.

It would be proper but perhaps impossible to acknowledge the numerous contributions individuals have played in helping accomplish this final document. Special recognition, however, is extended to Dr. James Dillehay, my friend and mentor; Dr. Vince Presno, for reading the manuscript and giving encouragement as well as constructive criticism; my wife, Kathy, for her patience and understanding; others too numerous to mention.

Joseph J. Cobb

CONTENTS

	Page
Preface	vii
Chapter 1—THE FEDERAL ROLE IN EDUCATION	3
Management and Control of Public Education	4
Sources of School Law	5
Constitutions	6
State Statutes	7
Judicial Opinions	8
Statutory Construction	8
The State Government and Education	9
The State Board	9
Chief State Officer	13
The Legal Status of the Local School District and School Board	14
Legal Responsibilities and Obligations of School Board	20
Legal Responsibilities of Teachers	20
The Legal Status of Public School Teachers	20
The First Amendment and Teachers' Rights	23
The Fifth Amendment	26
Rights Under the Fourteenth Amendment	29
Summary	33
Chapter 2—TENURE AND DISMISSAL	35
History of Tenure	35
In Defense of Tenure	40
Tenure and the Probationary Status	42
Tenure by Default, Acquiescence, or Estoppel	43

Tenure and Dismissal 44
Remedies for Dismissed Teachers 57
Summary 58

Chapter 3—CONTRACT OF EMPLOYMENT;
CERTIFICATION 60
Definition of Contracts 60
Elements of Contracts.......................... 62
Rights and Responsibilities After Employment ... 64
Dismissal Procedures 65
Certification 67
Summary...................................... 70

Chapter 4—TORT LIABILITY 76
Defenses to Tort.............................. 77
Statute of Limitations 77
Liability of School Districts for Negligence 78
Negligence 80
Defamation of Character 84
Control of Pupils' Conduct.................... 87
Miscellaneous Tort Cases 89
Summary...................................... 92

Chapter 5—STUDENT RIGHTS AND DUE PROCESS 98
Introduction 98
Reasons for Intervention 99
The Courts and Due Process.................... 100
Search and Seizure............................ 113
Hair Codes 119
Rights of Married Students 121
Due Process and the Schools.................... 123
Summary...................................... 129

Chapter 6—TEACHERS' CIVIL RIGHTS AND
RESPONSIBILITIES 132
The Modern View 134
Academic Freedom 134
Rights of Teachers Under Tenure 139

Teachers' Strikes 145

Summary 148

Chapter 7—CIVIL RIGHTS FOR THE HANDICAPPED ... 153

Introduction 153

Historical Perspective 154

PL 94-142—What It Is 156

Due Process and Least Restrictive Alternatives.... 157

Due Process Procedures for Parents and Children . 159

Summary 166

Appendix—Historical Highlights of Certification 179

Glossary 181

Index of Cases 185

Subject Index ....

An Introduction to Educational Law

Chapter 1

THE FEDERAL ROLE IN EDUCATION

Education in the United States operates within a well-defined legal structure, and each unit of the government exercises designated functions. Specific functions are the established province of the federal government, the state government, and the local government units, and the limitations are imposed on each unit. The guidelines for educational operations are established within a framework of constitutional provisions, charters, and statutory enactments.

The Federal Constitution covers a wide area of powers, duties, and limitations, but at no point does the Federal Constitution refer expressly to education. Thus, education becomes primarily a state function under the Tenth Amendment, which provides: "The powers not delegated to the United States by the Constitution nor prohibited by it to the states are reserved to the states respectively, or to the people."

It has been assumed that because of the power given to the states under the Tenth Amendment the federal government in no way relates to or controls education. Until recently the general public has been unaware of the extensive role the federal government plays in public education.

Actually, from the very beginning of our educational development, the federal government has assisted the state and local school systems by providing for educational opportunities. At first the assistance was provided conservatively and without noticeable control. "By 1965 the growing federalization of education had become so pronounced as to cause public attention

3

and concern throughout the nation."[1]

As an example, the Elementary and Secondary Education Act of 1965 provided federal funds to improve the education for poor children and to strengthen libraries, supplementary educational services, and state departments of education. In addition, the federal government had legislated monies for improving teacher training, curriculum development, teaching materials, and specialized training facilities. Although this federal aid is categorical rather than general, it is administered and controlled through several executive agencies such as the U. S. Office of Education and the National Science Foundation.

However, in virtually all congressional acts supporting public education, assuring statements are made that the control will remain with the state and local school systems. Realistically, however, local autonomy over all aspects of educational programs financed by the federal government will never result . . . "consequently the power of decision over public education is shifting rapidly from the local to the federal level.[2]

Federal involvement in education is based on the "general welfare" clause, article one, section ten of the United States Constitution, and the First, Fifth, and Fourteenth Amendments.

Article one, section ten of the U. S. Constitution authorizes congressional action on behalf of the people. The First Amendment protects freedom of speech, press, and religion, and the right of petition for redress of grievances. The Fifth Amendment addresses self-incrimination by teachers and pupils in school settings. The Fourteenth Amendment defines U. S. citizenship and bars state laws that abridge the privileges and immunities of such citizens and includes the right to "due process" and "equal protection of the laws."

Management and Control of Public Education

According to the Tenth Amendment of the Constitution, the management and control of public education is "primarily" a responsibility of the state. The United States Supreme Court has

---

[1]Bolmeier, Edward C.: *The School in the Legal Structure.* Cincinnati: The W. H. Anderson Company, 1973, p. 2.

[2]*Supra* note 1.

realized that the citizenry of a state should be educated at a certain level to maintain the purposes of education. To insure this end the Supreme Court has mandated that the states meet the educational responsibilities of the educational requirements by imposing certain limitations and guidelines on the states, thus . . .

> . . . it is of course, quite true that the responsibility for public education is "primarily" the concern of the states, but it is equally true that such responsibilities, like all other state activity, must be exercised consistently with federal constitutional requirements as they apply to state action.[3]

Subject to restrictions imposed by the state and federal constitutions, state legislatures create, fund, and regulate public schools through various state, intermediate, and local agencies. The state legislatures provide for the school's financial support, curriculum, qualifications of teachers, policies concerning pupils, and a vast range of school management policies and procedures. Most operational decisions are made by the local school boards, generally elected by and responsible to the voters in local school districts.

Subject to constitutional restrictions, the state legislature possesses plenary power over the public schools. "Plenary" means that the state has full or complete power to legislate or create the system of education it desires its citizens to have. Normally, this power is delegated to local boards of education. If it chooses to do so, the state legislature could redistrict local school boundaries, consolidate and/or abolish local school districts, prescribe curriculum, textbooks, school calendars, hours of school operation, and practically every other detail of school operation. This control by the state legislature is subject to review by the state courts, to the rights of citizens under the federal constitution, and to review by the federal courts for violation of constitutional rights.

Sources of School Law

Educators must be alert to the fact that legislation governing the operations of the public schools is ever-changing. As a

---

[3]Cooper v. Aaron, 358 U.S. 1, 78 Sup. Ct. 1401, 3 L. Ed. 2d 3 (Ark., 1963).

general rule, a law is to be regarded as an expression of current legislative policy, subject to change by later legislation. Fundamental to the *understanding of the law* applicable to the public school system is a realization that the rules of law that govern educational institutions come from many sources and in diverse forms. The law of any phase of government or society is found in constitutions, statutes, and judicial precedents; so too is "school law." When law is used in its specific meaning it refers to a body of legal rules that stem from a variety of sources: federal and state constitutions, federal and state statutes enacted by legislative bodies, state and local boards of education, and rules and regulations promulgated by state and federal administrative agencies.

It also relates to those principles established in the courts—the case law that rules by precedent. Other less known sources of law pertaining to education may include executive orders, municipal ordinances, and opinions issued by the Attorney General.

Constitutions

The Tenth Amendment to the Federal Constitution reserves to the states all matters not delegated to the Federal Government.

There are various reasons cited as to why education is not mentioned in the articles of the constitution. Some writers contend that since so many of those who helped draft the Constitution represented the old aristocracy, education was to be considered a private rather than public matter. Others contend that it was such a potentially explosive issue that it was omitted from the constitution because it would have jeopardized the acceptance of the document. "Still others have suggested that even the theory of education had not been thought out and formulated adequately enough at the time the constitution was framed to warrant provisions dealing with education."[4]

The first ten amendments to the Federal Constitution, known as the Bill of Rights, were adopted in the first years of the life of the Constitution. They were promulgated primarily to put upon the Federal Government certain restrictions because the patriots

---

[4]*Supra* note 1, p. 4.

of that day were afraid that the newly formed national government would take unto itself too much power. The Fourteenth Amendment made the restrictions of the first ten amendments applicable to the states. Hence, no state may violate any of the first ten amendments, even in an area such as education, which under the Tenth Amendment, is within the province of the state.

Within the boundaries of the Federal Constitution and statutory provisions, every state constitution contains some mention, at least, of public education. Some of the newer state constitutions contain many details concerning the public schools, while some of the older state constitutions are more general in their references. Almost all state constitutions contain some provisions regarding the financial support of the schools; two-thirds of them refer to the use of public funds in connection with the schools, school lands, higher education, and the office of the chief state school officer; half of them include provisions for local and county organization and administration, including local financial support; school age limits are established and state board of education is created by constitutional provisions in almost half of the states.

State Statutes

State statutes are a medium for regulating schools. State legislatures have enacted thousands of school laws; the statute books of every state contain legislation more or less extensively prescribing how the public schools shall be operated. State statutes enacted by legislatures are therefore the most prolific source of school law.

In any phase of school management wherein the state board of education has been given powers of operation, the rules and regulations of the state board have the force and effect of law. However, being a creature of the legislature in most states, the state board has only the powers delegated to it, implied in the delegated powers, or that it thinks it needs to accomplish its purposes. In states where the state board is created by constitutional provision, its constitutional powers are usually general, and in specific instances it depends upon the legislature for its authority to act. In either case, if the state board acts outside its delegated or implied powers, the rule or regulation is void. That is, however, a presumption of authority, and until challenged in court, all rules and regulations of the state board are presumed to be valid and are as enforceable as a statute by the legislature.

Judicial Opinions

Another source of school law lies in judicial opinions. Court decisions are primarily of two sorts: (1) interpretations of constitutional and statutory law and (2) the application of common law principles. The latter comes about when a particular set of circumstances has not been legislated upon and the rights of the parties must be decided by the court on the basis of general principles handed down traditionally over many years. One characteristic of the common law is the establishment of precedent. The doctrine is often called by its Latin name, *Stare decisis et non quieta movere,* "let the decision stand." The adherence to the doctrine provides for the likelihood of equality of treatment for all who come before the courts, contributes to predictability in future disputes, saves time and energy when principles are taken as established, and shows due respect for the experience and wisdom of prior generations of judges.

Most of our school law is based on statutory law. The common law does, however, come into the picture on some occasions.

Statutory Construction

The technical parts of a statute are the title, the preamble, the enacting clause, the body of the law, exceptions and provisos, interpreting clauses, and repealing and saving clauses.

Constitutional provisions in many states prohibit legislation that covers subject matter not included in the title. When the body of a law is broader than its title, the part outside the scope of the title is invalid; the part within the scope of the title is valid provided it can stand alone without the invalid part. If the parts of the statute are so interrelated that they cannot be separated without destroying the intent of the legislature, or if the separation leaves an absurdity, the whole act will fail.

The preamble is the preface at the beginning of a statute giving the reason for the enactment and the objectives to be accomplished by it. The preamble is not an essential part of a statute, and it is frequently omitted entirely.

The enacting clause is mere form: e.g., "Be it Enacted by the General Assembly Duly Convened." The repealing clause is some statement at the end, "All acts and parts of acts inconsistent herewith are hereby repealed."

The State Government and Education

The state government is a servant of the people. As long as it remains democratic, the people themselves shall decide the degrees of support and control of education by state governments and the federal government in accordance with the general welfare.

The original authority to establish, support, and govern schools is found in state constitutions. However, some early state constitutions contain no references to education or schools. State constitutions of New Hampshire, New Jersey, Delaware, Maryland, Virginia, South Carolina, New York, Kentucky, Tennessee, Louisiana, and Illinois—framed during the period from 1776 to 1818—all were equally silent on the matter of education.[5] Now each of the fifty states has included provisions for education in its constitution.

The State Board

A state board of education may be established by provisions of statute, constitutional enactment, or special charter. A state board of education may have broad or very limited powers depending on the breadth of legislative authorization. The limits of the authority and responsibilites of the state board are found in the respective state constitutions, statutes, and charters. In all but one state there is a state board of education having general authority over the public schools.

Powers delegated to a board by the state legislature cannot be

---

[5]Cubberly, Ellwood P.: *Public Education in the United States.* Chicago: Houghton Mifflin Co., 1934, p. 94.

redelegated or allocated by the board to others. In other words, the school board cannot give committees or employees or other governmental officials authority to perform acts over which the board has discretionary powers.[6]

A school board is the only agency in a community that is empowered by law to operate public schools. No other person or agency can operate a public school without the consent of the state board of education.

School boards (state and local) can exercise those powers that (1) are granted in expressed words, (2) can be fairly implied as necessary or incidental to powers expressly granted, and (3) are essential to realization of purposes of educational institutions.

Some general powers of state boards of education are that it may be placed in control of the state's public school system[7] and have power to determine general educational policy,[8] particularly policy related to teachers, curriculum, and supervision.[9]

The Legal Authority of State Boards

The legal authority of a state board of education is somewhat analogous to that of a local board of education—the main differences being that of geographic scope. The courts have rather uniformly held that education is essentially a state function rather than a local concern. The state board of education exercises authority over schools of the entire state, whereas the local board may exercise authority only over the schools of a designated territorial subdivision of the state school district.

Several methods of selecting the members of a state board of education are employed. The most common methods of selection are appointment by the governor. Election by popular vote is frequent. A few state board members get their posts ex-officio, election by school boards, and appointment by the state legislature.

Once the state board is established, it operates as an independent agency, and the appointing authorities have no veto

---

[6]Hamilton, Robert R. and E. Edmund Reutter: *Legal Aspects of School Board Operations*, New York: Teachers College, 1958, p. 6.
[7]Bell v. Board of Education, 215 S.W.2d 1007 (Ky. 1948).
[8]Board of Education v. Goodpaster, 84 S.W2d 55 (Ky. 1935).
[9]Board of Education v. Rogers, 15 N.E.2d 401 (N.Y. 1938).

power over the board. The board decisions are final and conclusive and not subject to review. The courts, however, are not deprived of jurisdiction on the legal questions that may arise in connection with the educational statutes.

The origin of the office of school board member is by constitutional enactment, statutes, and charters. In other words, the position is a creature of the legislature. In the absence of any constitutional provision to the contrary, the legislature is free to provide for any kind of administrative machine to operate its public schools that it sees fit. It may create the position of school board member; having done so, it is free to abolish the office, change its term, or make any other changes as it sees fit.

Term of Office

The term of office for state school board member ranges from two to thirteen years. There is no uniform number of years a board may serve per state. A six year term of office is the most common, as found in fifteen of the states. Some of the laws establish the term of office so that they overlap, in order to provide stability and continuity for state educational programs and prohibiting an entirely new board from taking office in any one year.

Size of Boards

The number of members on a state board of education ranges from three to twenty-three. Many laws dictate a board must not be an even number board to preclude a possibility of a stalemate in voting.

Recommendations for State Boards

The following recommendations with reference to state boards were made by Cubberley in 1927 and are worth repeating. He recommended that the state board of education should be—

1. A lay board representing the people.
2. Neither too small nor too large, with seven members as optimum size.

3. Appointed or elected for relatively long and overlapping terms.
4. Appointed by a governor who does not have opportunity to change the entire character of the board during one term.
5. Appointed solely on the basis of ability to serve the people without reference to race, creed, occupation, party, and residence.
6. Elected by the people if this is preferred to appointment.
7. Removed only by action of the governor and then only for such causes as immorality, malfeasance, and gross incompetence.
8. Without ex-officio members, even the governor.
9. Organized so that the state superintendent is not a member of the board.
10. Paid an honorarium instead of a per diem allotment.
11. Able to consider as its most important function the appointment of a state superintendent.
12. Organized in such a way that the subordinate officials for the state department are selected only on the recommendations of the state superintendent.
13. Empowered to make its own rules and regulations.
14. Organized so that there is a clear distinction between the legislative and the executive functions.[10]

Duties of the State Board of Education

The duties of the State Board of Education should be defined in state statutes. Some of these duties are to—

1. Formulate policies and adopt such rules and regulations as are necessary to carry out the responsibilities assigned to it by the state constitution and statutes of the state.
2. Appoint and fix the salaries of the professional staff of the state department of education on the recommendation of the chief state school officer.
3. Establish standards for issuance and revocation of teacher certification.
4. Establish standards for classifying, approving, and accrediting schools, both public and non-public.
5. Prescribe a uniform system for the gathering and reporting

---

[10]*Supra* note 5, p. 290-294.

of educational data, for the keeping of adequate educational and finance records, and for the better evaluation of educational progress.

6. Submit an annual report to the governor and legislature covering the areas of action of the state board of education and the operations of the state department of education and to support education throughout the state.

7. Consider the educational needs of the state and recommend to the governor and the legislature such additional legislation or changes in existing legislation as it may deem desirable.

8. Interpret its own rules and regulations and upon appeal hear all controversies and disputes arising therefrom.

9. Publish the laws relating to education with notes and comments for the guidance of those charged with the educational responsibility.

10. Provide through the state department of education supervisory and consultative service and issue materials which would be helpful in the development of educational programs.

11. Accept and distribute in accord with the law any monies, commodities, goods, and services which may be made available from the state or federal government or from other sources.

12. Designate the extent to which the board is empowered to exercise supervision over public and non-public colleges, universities, state institutions and public and non-public elementary and secondary schools in accord with the law and sound public policy on education.[11]

Chief State Officer

The Council of Chief State School Officers recommended that the state legislature enact laws defining the relation of the chief state school officer to the state board of education and to the state department of education. These laws should indicate the functions of the chief state school officer in a general way, namely—

---

[11]National Council of Chief State School Officers: *The State Department of Education.* Washington, D.C.: The Council, 1952, p. 14-16.

1. Keeping the board currently advised about the operations and status of the public schools.
2. Recommending to the board such policies and rules as he deems necessary for educational progress.
3. Serving as executive officer of the board and being responsible for promoting efficiency and improvement in the public school system.
4. Delegating ministerial and executive functions to members of the state department of education.
5. Preparing a budget for the state education program under the jurisdiction of the state education agency, including the state department of education, and administering the same after approval.
6. Establishing and maintaining a system of personnel administration.[12]

The Legal Status of the Local School District and School Board

Local school districts are territorial divisions of a state created for the express purpose of operating public schools. Sometimes the area is coterminous with a city or town, but the government is separate to a large extent, if not entirely.

In some states school districting has been abandoned in favor of the county unit, in which case the entire county is a single school district and the governing agency is a county body. On the other hand, some large cities contain more than one school district. Arrangements, therefore, differ from state to state, and even within states there are frequently differences depending upon the size or class of city or political division. The public schools are operated in subdivisions of the state that are usually legally separate from other civil units.

The governing authority is called the school board, the board of trustees, the board of education, the school committee, etc. The school district and the school board are state agencies and are subject to the will of the state legislature and the state educational authorities, except in those matters left to local discretion.

Since education is a function of the state and not local

---

[12]*Supra* note 11, p. 16.

government, it follows that school officers, e.g. members of a local board of education, are state and not local officers.[13] In this connection, it has been held that the fact that "the legislature has seen fit to vest the power of appointment and of removal . . . (school board) members in (a city official such as) the Mayor . . . cannot affect the status of the board as an agency of state government" and that the mayor, "in exercising his appointive and removal powers . . . is acting . . . as a state officer in support of the state system of education."[14]

School districts, unlike cities, which are pure municipal corporations, are quasi-municipal corporations.[15]

It has been held that a school district or a school board is a body politic and corporate[16] with authority to sue and be sued in some states,[17] but without such authority in others.[18] A school district is a separate corporate entity, distinct and free from the government of the municipality except to the extent that the legislature has provided for connection or interdependence.

Contracts, title to property, and other business is carried on in the corporate name of the school district—not in the names of the members of the board. If there is liability on the part of the school board, it is the board itself, not its individual members, that is responsible. However, it has been held that, under certain circumstances, individual board members may be held personally liable for the legal expenditure of public funds. While he will not be held accountable for loss of funds because of his negligence or poor judgment, he may be liable if funds are expended in clear violation of the law. The liability in the latter situation is founded on the principle that it is a dereliction of duty for a board to spend public funds in violation of the law.[19]

The local school district is a quasi-municipal corporation. It is also a civil subdivision of the state whose boundaries, and the

---

[13]Lanza v. Wagner, 11 N.Y.2d 317, 183 N.E.2d 670.

[14]*Supra* note 13.

[15]Ludwig v. Board of Education, 183 N.E.2d 32 (Ill.); People v. Furman, 186 N.E.2d 262 (Ill.).

[16]Wilder v. Board of Education, 230 N.Y.S.2d 973.

[17]Board of Education v. Marting, 185 N.E.2d 597 (Ohio).

[18]Mormon v. Board of Education, 126 S.E.2d 217 (Ga.).

[19]Simpson, Robert J. (Editor): *Education and the Law in Ohio.* Cincinnati: The W. H. Anderson Company, 1968, p. 54.

procedures for altering such boundaries, are determined by state law. It is concerned specifically with the state's function of education. Only the school board has the legal authority to determine salary and working conditions for teachers.

It is well established that the school board can exercise those powers that (1) are granted in express words, (2) can be fairly implied as necessary or incidental to powers expressly granted, and (3) are essential to realization of purposes of educational institutions. The board cannot employ discretionary powers to create authority not intended by law or to ignore demands of the state code or regulations that are properly the legal domain of the state department of public instruction.

Significant Responsibilities of the Local Board

The significant responsibilities of the local school board can be summarized as follows:

1. To satisfy the spirit as well as the word of state laws dealing with education and of the regulations of the state education authority.
2. To ascertain goals or objectives of public education and to prepare general policies in tune with them.
3. To select a superintendent of schools, designate him as chief executive officer, and work harmoniously with him.
4. To strive continuously to develop further and improve the scope and quality of educational opportunities for all children and youth in the district.
5. To create policies which will attract and retain professional and other personnel needed to realize educational objectives.
6. To provide educationally efficient and safe school plant facilities.
7. To plan for and obtain financial resources necessary to achieve educational goals.
8. To keep the people of the district informed and aware of status, progress, and problems of their schools.
9. To appraise activities of the school district in the light of its objectives.
10. To discharge its responsibilities as a state agency by participating in statewide efforts to promote and improve public education.[20]

---

[20]Knezevich, S.J. and H.C. DeKoch: *The Iowa School Board Member.* Des Moines. Iowa: Iowa Association of School Boards, 1960. p. 17-18.

Policy Making

Policy making is judged to be a most important function of a board of education. A local board of education is the only body that legally can make policy. Policy cannot be made by any body or institution subordinate to the board of education. A board of education cannot delegate this function to any body or institution.

A policy is a general statement of intent to act in a particular manner when confronted with a given situation or to achieve a given result at some future point in time. A policy statement represents a guideline to future courses of action to be pursued to ensure consistency and fairness.[21] Policy making is (1) the act of establishing principles to serve as guides for action and (2) a function of an individual or body of individuals legally endowed with the authority or to whom has been delegated the responsibility to establish policies.[22]

Policy formulation is a function of policy making that has to do with the selection and statement of the principles and rules of action that are to govern a particular type of activity.[23] A policy statement may be broad or specific, cover many dimensions or one dimension of an issue, or simply define limits to be observed in reaching a decision on a given matter.

Rules and regulations grow out of policy and should be consistent with announced policy. In essence, if there is no policy under which rules and regulations can fit, there should be no rules or regulations governing conduct or action of people. A policy is a general statement that serves as a guideline to future action. A rule or regulation is a detailed activity and establishes specific directions for implementation of policy. All policies, to be effective, should be reduced to writing.

Value of Policy

Policies are valuable to a school board and district because—

---

[21]Knezivich, S.J.: *Administration of Public Education.* New York: Harper and Row, 1975, p. 321.

[22]Good, Carter, Victor: *Dictionary of Education.* New York: McGraw-Hill, 1973, p. 428.

[23]*Supra* note 22.

1. They help clarify responsibilities among board, administrative staff, teaching staff, and community.
2. They help promote more consistent and prudent decision-making, or stated negatively, they minimize embarrassing inconsistencies in school board action.
3. They provide continuity of action.
4. They can save the board time, money and effort, for many specific questions deal with similar principles, that is, repeat themselves in a variety of forms, and therefore can be handled in a manner suggested by a single policy.
5. They can help improve public relations.
6. They help reduce criticism of board action when it becomes apparent to the community that board decisions are based on well-defined and consistent policies rather than on expediency.
7. They help reduce pressure on the board from special-interest pleaders.
8. They give the board a sense of direction.
9. They facilitate orderly review of board practices.
10. They ensure a better informed board and staff.[24]

Content of Policy Statements

There is no conformity of what should be covered in policy statements. Policy statements differ from district to district. However, policy statements should encompass all aspects of school operation that command the attention of the school board. School board policies normally include:

1. Legal status, functions, organization, and ethical conduct of the board of education.
2. Selection, retention, and duties of the chief executive officer or superintendent of schools.
3. Relations among personnel in the school system.
4. Scope and quality of the instructional program and school services within the system.
5. Function and operation of the school food services.
6. Procedures and other aspects of budgeting, accounting, auditing, and management of school property.
7. Operation of the pupil transportation system.

---

[24]American Association of School Administrators and National School Boards Association: *Written Policies for School Boards.* Washington, D.C.: The Association, 1955, p. 6.

8. Selection, retention, and other matters related to the professional personnel.
9. Selection, retention, and other matters related to the non-professional personnel.
10. Identification, admission, promotion, discipline, etc. of pupils.
11. Public relations.[25]

Local School Board Meetings

School boards normally have the authority to hold their meetings to suit the convenience of the members. In some states, the time and place is specified in statute. Most school boards meet about twice a month on the date set by the membership. Some will meet once monthly, or call additional meetings as necessary. School board meetings are normally held at night. In some districts, meetings are held early mornings, noon, afternoons, etc. There is no set time stipulated by statute.

MINUTES OF BOARD MEETINGS. School board minutes are public records and are open to examination by taxpayers or by other persons who have good reasons to examine them. The minutes become official records when formally approved by the board and signed by the secretary and the president of the board.

Local School Board Composition

The size of the local school board is dictated by state statute. The size of local boards range from three to nineteen members. Normally, a local board is constituted of five to seven members. Local school board members serve a specified term. In most states there are no statutory limitations on the number of successive terms a person can serve. Local school board members are elected at-large or appointed to their position. Most members serve a four year term if elected and a five year term if appointed. Any qualified voter is eligible for board membership in most school districts.

---

[25]*Supra* note 24.

Legal Responsibilities and Obligations of School Board

The school board should support teachers in their endeavors to be professionals; carry to the highest level the development and learning of every student; strengthen in every possible way the intellectual, social, and cultural well-being of the community as a whole; and equalize educational opportunities and access to it.[26]

In addition, school boards should assure that programs are relevant to the public interest and the requirements of the modern world, and that their procedures are effective in accomplishing their purposes.

Legal Responsibilities of Teachers

The professional who voluntarily serves in the school accepts as a condition of his employment the obligation to help maintain and improve the institution in which he serves.

In regard to all professional employees, three peculiar characteristics of a professional should be recognized by all concerned with the work of the school. One is that every practitioner is personally and legally responsible for the quality of his judgment and his performance as a professional and for the consequences of his own acts. The second is that no group can expect to enjoy the full status of a profession unless it is willing and able to establish and enforce standards of competence among its members. The third characteristic is the obligation of the profession collectively and as individuals to serve the public interest and promote the welfare of its clients.[27]

The Legal Status of Public School Teachers

The position of the public school teacher is created by legislatures directly and by the state constitutions indirectly in provisions requiring the legislature to establish and maintain public schools. The powers and duties of public school

---

[26]Elam, Lieverman and Moslow: *Negotiations in Public Education*. Chicago: Rand McNally Co., 1967, p. 25.

[27]*Supra* note 26, p. 25.

teachers are fixed by law to a large extent. Some people contend that public school teachers are public officers rather than employees. A distinction between employees and officers is important because if teachers were school officers, their status would be materially affected by the body of law dealing with public officers rather than public employees.

The elements said to be dispensable in any public office are:

1. It must be created by the constitution or by the legislature or created by a municipality or other body through authority conferred by the legislature.
2. It must possess a delegation of a portion of the sovereign power of government to be exercised for the benefit of the public.
3. The powers conferred, and the duties to be discharged must be defined directly or implied by the legislature or through legislative authority.
4. The duties must be performed independently and without control of a superior power, other than the law, unless they be those of an inferior or subordinate office, created or authorized by the legislature, or by it placed under the general control of a superior office or body.
5. It must have some permanency and continuity, and not only be temporary or occasional.[28]

There are many characteristics of the public school teacher that suggest that the position is a public office. A number of courts, however, have held that the most important and decisive difference is that "employment does not authorize the exercise in one's own right of any sovereign power or any prescribed independent authority of a governmental nature."[29]

Certification and Appointment

A teacher's certificate is a document indicating that the holder has met the legal requirements to follow the teaching profession. Holding a teacher's certificate does not by itself give the holder a right to demand a position except in rare

---

[28]State *ex rel.* Barney v. Hawkins, 79 Mont. 506, 257 Pac. 411 (Montana 1927).
[29]State *ex rel.* Halloway v. Sheats, 78 Fla. 583, 83 So. 508 (Florida 1919).

instances. In addition to professional qualifications, there are frequently personal standards that must be met in order to qualify for a certificate:

1. Citizenship
2. Age
3. Good moral character
4. Adequate physical condition

Today most certificates are granted on the basis of professional preparation. The state department of education or an agency therein is usually made the exclusive certifying authority in the state, and the certificates it issues are valid throughout the entire state. Ordinarily, the school board must employ a teacher; in only a few states may the board delegate this authority to the superintendent. If there is no statutory authority for such delegation, employment by the superintendent may not be legal. In that event, the board is not bound by the superintendent's selection.

Teachers' Salaries

Salary is the issue most commonly sought to be settled by collective negotiations, and dissatisfaction with salaries is most often the controversy resulting in teacher's strikes. The salary a teacher is to be paid usually is and certainly always should be named in the employment contract. Many districts have adopted salary schedules in which teachers are classified and salary is stated for each class with increments of specific amounts due at stated times. Salary schedules are usually matters of local regulations but some are statewide statutes.

In times of economic stress, a local board has the right to modify or abolish its salary schedule. Teachers have no vested rights in the increments set up on the schedule. The general principle is that a salary schedule does not create vested rights for the future. If a board makes the downward modification before contracts for the coming year are issued (or before the ensuing school year begins in the event that written contracts are not issued annually), such modification is legal. However, after contracts for the ensuing school year have been issued (or after the ensuing year has begun), such modification is an impairment of an accrued right of the teachers.

The First Amendment and Teachers' Rights

One of the major guarantees of individual rights found in the United States Constitution is contained in the First Amendment. This amendment, having far-reaching influence both upon private individuals and upon the educational system, provides that "Congress shall make no law respecting an establishment of religion, or prohibiting the free exercise thereof; or abridging the freedom of speech or of the press; or of the right of the people to peaceably assemble, and to petition the government for a redress of grievances."

The first part of this amendment "Congress shall make no law respecting an establishment of religion, or prohibiting the free exercise thereof" applied only to Congress and not to state legislatures; i.e., "Congress shall make no law." However, United States Supreme Court interpretations have established that this prohibition is applicable to the states, the legal link being provided by the Fourteenth Amendment, which provides that "No state shall make or enforce any law which shall abridge the privileges and immunities of citizens of the United States."[30]

Like all other constitutional rights, the right of assembly or association does not exist without limitation. For example, the word "peaceably" as cited in the First Amendment assures that the right is not absolute. Because of the very nature of the teaching profession, where the influence of the teacher is most extraordinary in developing our future citizens, the teacher may be more limited in his association than are persons in other professions or vocations.

In 1969 the Supreme Court of the United States in Tinker[31] decided that teachers and students have First Amendment rights in the classroom, but they are limited in many cases because of the "special characterictics of the school environment." To ascertain what limitations the state could place on the freedom of teachers and pupils under the First Amendment, the courts ruled it must be shown that such . . . "Action was caused by something more than a mere desire to avoid an unpopular viewpoint. . . ."[32] Such

---

[30]Cantwill v. Connecticut, 310 U.S. 296, 60 Sup. Ct. 900, 84 L.Ed. 1213 (Conn. 1940); Everson v. Board of Education, 330 U.S. 1, 67 Sup. Ct. 504, 91 L. Ed. 711 (N.Y. 1947).

[31]Tinker Independent School District, 393 U.S. 503 (1969).

[32]*Supra* note 31, at 509.

action must be necessary, because the exercise of the forbidden right would "materially and substantially interfere with the requirement of appropriate discipline in the operation of the school."[33]

A large array of cases involving teachers' rights under the First Amendment have come before the Supreme Court. These cases will be discussed as they bear upon specific topics treated in other chapters. However, the following cases will be cited to indicate the power a school board possesses to limit a teacher's freedom of expression.

The board of education in East Hartford, Connecticut, promulgated a dress code that required male classroom teachers to wear jacket, shirt, and tie. The plaintiff teacher sought an injunction restraining the board from enforcing the dress code on the grounds that it infringes on his protected interest in "personal liberty" in dressing as he pleases. The plaintiff claimed the board may not restrain his personal liberty in this fashion unless the board shows that his dressing as he pleases "would materially or substantially interfere with the requirements of appropriate discipline for the proper administration of the school."[34]

The court held that a dress code does not unconstitutionally restrain the liberty of an individual and thus it is within the discretion of the board to require some formality of dress. The court expressed its views as follows:

> Teachers set an example in dress and grooming for their students to follow. A teacher who understands this precept and adheres to it enlarges the importance of the task of teaching, presents an image of dignity and encourages respect for authority, which acts as a positive factor in maintaining classroom discipline.[35]

In *Pickering v. Board of Education*, the U.S. Supreme Court reversed a judgment of the Supreme Court of Illinois, which had upheld the dismissal of a teacher (Pickering) by the school board for sending a letter to a local newspaper concerning a recently

---

[33]Burnside v. Byars, 363 F.2d 744 (Fifth Cir. 1966).

[34]East Hartford Education Association v. Board of Education of Town of East Hartford, 405 F. Supp. 94 (D. Conn. 1975), 96.

[35]*Supra* note 34, p. 98. (discussed in *Yearbook of School Law*. Topeka, Kansas: NOLPE, 1976, 161-162).

proposed tax increase. The letter severely criticized the school board and the superintendent for the manner in which they had previously handled proposals to raise and use new revenue.

The board dismissed the teacher for writing the letter, which allegedly contained false statements, claiming that it damaged the reputations of board members and the school administrators.

In a ruling in favor of the teacher, the United States Supreme Court ruled in part: "Teachers are, as a class, the members of a community most likely to have informed and definite opinions as to how funds alloted to the operation of the schools should be spent. Accordingly, it is essential that they be able to speak freely on such questions without fear of retaliatory dismissal."[36]

First Amendment Rights

The Tenth Circuit Court in 1975 upheld the nonrenewal of a teacher's contract despite her claim that it was not renewed in retaliation for First Amendment activities.[37] She had appeared on a local radio show and had criticized the school's dress code at a time when the school board was attempting to negotiate a new dress code with members of the student government. After her appearance on the program, the superintendent reminded the plaintiff that she was up for tenure and that he was not certain that he wanted a teacher who did not support the school's policies. The court upheld the dismissal.

Free Speech

A principal who wrote rather untempered letters to the board of education was not protected by any right of free speech since harmony between a principal and the school board is a legitimate educational interest of the state, which outweighs the principal's right to free speech in these circumstances.[38]

Free speech under the First Amendment does not protect a teacher who publically advocates gay rights from submitting to a

---

[36]Pickering v. Board of Education, 391 U.S. 563, 20 L. Ed. 2d. 811, 88 sup. Ct. 1736 (1968).
[37]Bertot v. School District Number 1, 522 F.2d 1171 (10th Cir. 1975).
[38]Rost v. Horky, 422 F. Supp. 615 (D. Nlb. 1976).

board-ordered psychiatric examination in New Jersey.[39]

Freedom of Association

In Georgia, a federal district court held that a school board's denial of employment to a resident of a communal farm violated her right to free association.[40] She had previously served as a substitute in the district and her effectiveness was not in question. The court ordered the board of education to hire the teacher for the first appropriate position that became vacant.

The Fifth Amendment

Generally a public school teacher possesses certain freedoms enjoyed by all citizens. As a citizen he has the right to speak, think, and behave as he wishes. He may, with rare exceptions, affiliate with groups of his choice. As a public school teacher he must exercise these and other legal rights with restricted discretion, and with due consideration of the effect upon others, especially school children. Moreover, by virtue of his position, performing a governmental function, he must conform to certain laws, rules, and regulations not equally applicable to citizens outside the teaching profession.

It is generally agreed that the individual rights protected by the Fifth Amendment are not absolute and are subject to reasonable governmental limitation and regulation. Using this rationale, it has been held that a board of education may limit the freedom of teachers guaranteed under the Fifth Amendment to the United States Constitution.

The two most frequent areas of litigation under the Fifth Amendment are "Loyalty Oaths" and "Pleading the Fifth."

---

[39]Gish v. Board of Education of Borough of Paramus, 366 A.2d 1337 (N.J. Super. Ct. 1976).

[40]Dottery v. Wilson, 356 F. Supp. 35 (M.D. Ga. 1973); *also see Contemporary Legal Problems in Education:* Topeka Kansas: NOLPE, 1975; *Yearbook of School Law.* Topeka, Kansas: NOLPE, 1974, at 114.

Loyalty Oaths

One of the early decisions of the U.S. Supreme Court involving loyalty oaths is *Wieman v. Updegraff*,[41] one of the court's few loyalty cases in which the decision was unanimous. In essence, the statute required public employees, including teachers, to subscribe to an oath affirming that they were not affiliated with, and during the past five years had not been a member of, any organization determined by the U.S. Attorney General to be "subversive." The statute was upheld by the state courts, but the U.S. Supreme Court held that the statute violated the due process clause of the Federal Constitution, because it was limited to public employees who joined or were affiliated with "subversive" organizations knowing them to be subversive. The Court stated that, in all loyalty oath statutes that had been upheld, scienter (knowledge of the facts) was required either by implication or by state court interpretation. The legal principle to be drawn (Updegraff) is that, in the interest of protecting its public schools from subversive influence, a state may exclude from public school employment persons who are or who have been members or affiliates of subversive organizations but may not exclude them if, after notice and opportunity to be heard, it is determined that the organizations are subversive and such persons knew they were subversive.

The loyalty oaths and related board rules, with some exceptions, have been upheld by the courts. Loyalty oath laws generally are attacked on two bases: (a) the claim that the oath and related questions violate the Fifth Amendment and (b) the oath and consequences of refusal to make it violate the due process clause of the Federal Constitution, because it was not limited to public employees who joined or were affiliated with "subversive" interest in education and qualifications of teachers justifies reasonable efforts to deny employment to and remove from public employment those who are committed to the overthrow of

---

[41]Wieman v. Updegraff, 344 U.S. 183, 195 (1952).

the federal or state government. In general, states may require loyalty oaths of public school personnel so long as the content and penalties prescribed do not violate due process under the federal and state constitutions.

Pleading the Fifth Amendment

Closely related to the problems arising out of loyalty oaths and subversive organizations are the problems incidental to the exercise by teachers of their constitutional right to plead the Fifth Amendment. This amendment provides in part that (no person). . . shall be compelled in any criminal case to be a witness against himself, nor be deprived of life, liberty, or property, without due process of law. . . .

Statutes in several states provide for the automatic dismissal of public employees, including teachers, who exercise this constitutional privilege and refuse to answer questions put to them in hearings before federal or state investigating committees. In several decisions upholding dismissals for exercising the privilege against self-incrimination, teachers have contended that such dismissals violate their constitutional privilege to refuse to remain silent. The courts have answered by saying that a teacher has a constitutional privilege to refuse to answer but not a constitutional right to remain a teacher in public education.

However, using Slochower[42] and Konigsberg,[43] the court has ruled that a public school teacher may not be dismissed solely because he exercises his constitutional right of refusing to answer a question put to him by a federal or state legislative committee. However, it is ground for dismissal for such teacher to refuse to answer similar questions when put to him by his school superintendent or to explain to the superintendent why he exercised his constitutional right before the legislative committee.

It is the refusal to answer the superintendent—because of his obligation to be frank, candid, and cooperative—that constitutes grounds for dismissal.

---

[42]Slochower v. Board of Education, 350 U.S. 558.
[43]Konigsberg v. State Bar of California, 353 U.S. 252.

In essence, the courts have held that school boards have the right to remove teachers who refuse to testify. Even though teachers may be required to answer questions concerning their own affiliation with the Communist party, they may not be required to disclose the names of other presently employed teachers known to be or to have been members.[44]

Rights Under the Fourteenth Amendment

The Fourteenth Amendment is commonly referred to as "Due Process Amendment." Due process includes two distinct aspects: "substantive" and "procedural."

It is difficult to define due process since the courts have been hesitant to set forth any specific, absolute, and final definition. Over the years the federal judges have indicated that due process was a "fairness" for the individual and that "fairness" in one instance was not necessarily "fairness" in all cases. Due process is met when the principles of fair play are involved and when actions are reasonable, just, and not arbitrary.[45] Due process requires no fixed set of procedures as long as the principles of liberty and justice are preserved, and the "decencies of civilized conduct" is followed;[46] therefore, it is not a technical conception with a fixed content unrelated to time, place, and circumstances. Due process is not a mechanical instrument. It is not a yardstick. It is a delicate process of adjustment.[47] In essence, due process is decided case by case.

SUBSTANTIVE DUE PROCESS: Substantive due process involves protection specifically listed in the constitution and the Bill of Rights, such rights as freedom of speech, association, and religion.

PROCEDURAL DUE PROCESS: Procedural due process involves the right to a fair procedure to determine the necessity for depriving an individual of substantive rights, life, liberty, or property.

---

[44]*Supra* note 1, p. 214-215.

[45]*Yearbook of Higher Education Law.* Topeka, Kansas: NOLPE, 1977, p. 62.

[46]Hurtado v. California, 110 U.S. 516 (1884); Rochin v. California, 342 U.S. 165 (1952).

[47]Joint Anti-Fascist Committee v. McGrath, 341 U.S. 123 (1951).

Property or Liberty Under Due Process

The question of whether teachers have protected property or liberty interests that entitle them to full due process hearings before termination continues to be litigated at great length. Generally, untenured teachers do not have a property interest, though it is possible to find one on the basis of special circumstances, such as the wording of a state statute or a collective bargaining agreement. There is some faint indication in some of the language that even tenured teachers do not always have a property interest. The liberty interest revolves around the earlier established standards that publicity may curtail a teacher's "liberty" for purposes of acquiring due process rights, but not unless the teacher is stigmatized, which means that the public comments go to the heart of the teacher's competency.[48]

Establishing a Property Interest

A case that construed a state statute to find no property interest was established concerned a principal who was reassigned to teaching duties without a hearing. The court ruled that tenure can only be acquired for the status of "certified employee" not the for principalship. Thus, in Illinois, a principal may be reassigned without notice and a hearing to a teaching position at a reduced salary as long as the action is done in good faith and not to subvert the provisions of the school code.

The delay in the notice of termination of a probationary teacher was ruled to create a property interest for Fourteenth Amendment purposes.[49]

Procedural due process is required by the Fourteenth Amendment when the government seeks to deprive any person of life, liberty, or property.

"Property for Fourteenth Amendment purposes normally obtains its content by reference to local law."[50] For an employee to be able to claim a "property" right and "due process" as it relates to public employment, one must be able to establish a

---

[48]See *The Yearbook of School Law*. Topeka, Kansas: NOLPE, 1977, p. 189.
[49]Turano v. Board of Education of Island Trees, 411 F. Supp. 205 (E.D. N.Y. 1976).
[50]Lipp v. Board of Education of City of Chicago, 479 F.2d 802 (7th Cir., 1972).

legitimate claim to it.[51] This claim must be made under the laws of the state, and the employee has the burden of showing some form of entitlement to that position. It has been held that one has no inherent right to a teaching position. One has only the privilege of being employed. However, the courts have ruled that when tenure has been conferred a property right exists and that right affords constitutional protection.[52]

In the case of teachers who go on strike, the courts have ruled that striking teachers do not have due process rights where termination of striking employees is authorized by state statute.

In defining "liberty" interest, the courts have said that the "liberty" protected by the Fourteenth Amendment must be asserted in the federal courts rather than in the state courts as the deprivation of a liberty interest can only result from a governmental action that infringes on one's liberty rights.[53]

In defining liberty interest, the courts have said that the liberty protected by the Fourteenth Amendment includes:

1. the person's good name;
2. the person's reputation;
3. the person's honor;
4. the person's integrity, or if the state damage a person's standing in the community by charging him with an unsavory character trait such as dishonesty or immorality.[54]

Where charges are made that might raise a liberty interest such as to require procedural due process, the charges must be made public and not merely be presented in a confidential file.[55]

Restrictions Under the Due Process of Law

A clause in the Fourteenth Amendment provides that no state shall "deprive any person of life, liberty, or property, without due process of law." As this amendment is now interpreted, the

---

[51]Gotkin v. Miller, 514 F.2d 125 (2d Cir., 1975); *also see* Lampshire, Richard H.: *Current Legal Issues in Education.* Topeka, Kansas: NOLPE, 1976, p. 53.

[52]Collins v. Wolfson, 498 F.2d 1100 (5th Cir., 1974).

[53]Calvin v. Rupp, 471 F.2d 1346 (8th Cir., 1972); Tichon v. Harder, 438 F.2d 1396 (2d Cir., 1971). *Also see* Lampshire, *supra* note 51, at 56.

[54]Hostrop v. Board of Junior College District 515, 471 F.2d 488 (7th Cir., 1972).

[55]Kaprelilan v. Texan Women's University, 509 F.2d (5th Cir., 1975). *Also see* Lampshire, *supra* note 51, at 59.

Supreme Court of the United States exercises final determination of what constitutes proper exercise of the police power on the part of the states. Police power is that power of the state to limit individual rights in the interest of the social group. Rights of person and of property may be restricted in any manner and to any extent reasonably necessary to promote public health, morals, comfort, and the general welfare. Even rights guaranteed by the constitution are subject to limitation under the police power of the state.[56]

The police power is inherent in every state and it is a prerogative of the state legislature to determine for what purposes and in what manner it shall be exercised. There are, however, limits to the exercise of the police power; the individual has certain fundamental rights that must be respected.[57]

Although the police power is inherent in the legislature, the legislature itself is not the final judge of the limits to which the state may go in the curtailment of individual rights. The court of final jurisdiction in any state may nullify a statute as an arbitrary exercise of police power; even when a statute is sustained by the state courts, it may be declared invalid by the Supreme Court of the United States as being in violation of the due process of law clause.

Hearings

Hearings by boards of education are civil proceedings and, therefore, need not contain all the judicial safeguards required in criminal proceedings. To afford minimum protection in instances where a teacher is entitled to a hearing, the Federal Court of Appeals for the Fifth Circuit has listed the following requirements:

    a. He be advised of the cause or causes for his termination in sufficient detail to fairly enable him to show any error that may exist.

    b. He be advised of the names and the nature of the testimony of witnesses against him.

---

[56]See Newtone, Edwards: *Courts and the Public Schools.* Chicago: The University of Chicago Press, 1955, p. 11-12.

[57]*Supra* note 56, p. 13.

c. At a reasonable time after such advice, he must be accorded a meaningful opportunity to be heard in his own defense.

d. The hearing be before a tribunal that possesses some academic expertise and has an apparent impartiality toward the charges.[58]

Summary

Public education in the United States is a matter of federal interest, a state function, and a local operation. Our political system makes each state responsible for the organization and administration of education. Education becomes a state function under the Tenth Amendment, which provides: "The powers not delegated to the United States by the Constitution, nor prohibited by it to the States, are reserved to the States respectively, or to the people."

School boards are quasi-corporate bodies, created by state law to exercise certain delegated powers over local schools. The board's power extends over the school district for which it is constituted. The local school board acts as the state's agent for public education. Most school boards consist of members elected by the district voters. This means that board members may be regarded as dual representatives—agents of the state and of the voters.

School boards hold three kinds of power: (1) express power granted by law, (2) implied power arising from the express, and (3) those powers reasonably necessary to achieve the purposes of the granted powers.

The First Amendment rests upon the premise that both religion and government can best work to achieve their lofty aims if each is left free from the other within its respective sphere.

As interpreted by the courts, "equal protection" means the protection of equal laws, not the concept of "equality of people."

Federal Provisions Most Commonly Used in Educational Law

Article I. Section 8: General Welfare Clause

"The Congress shall have the power to lay and collect Taxes,

---

[58]Ferguson v. Thomas, 430 F.2d 852 (5th Cir., 1970). *Also see, supra* note 45, p. 68.

Duties, Imposts and Exercise, to pay the Debts and provide for the common Defence and general welfare of the United States."

Scope and Power:

". . . They (Congress) are not to lay taxes and libitum for any purpose they please but only to pay the debts or provide for the general welfare of the Union. . . . The federal Congress is authorized to levy taxes for the purpose of providing financial support for education, but it is not authorized to direct or control education."

Article I, Section 10: Impairment of Contracts

"No state shall . . . pass any Bill of Attainder, ex post facto Law, or Law impairing the Obligation of Contracts."

First Amendment

"Congress shall make no law respecting an establishment of religion, or prohibiting the free exercise thereof . . . Or abridging the freedom of speech . . . Or the right of the people peacably to assemble . . ."

Fifth Amendment

"No person shall be . . . deprived of life, liberty, or property without due process of law . . . nor shall be compelled in any criminal case to be witness against himself . . . in any proceedings in which testimony is legally required, persons may refuse to answer any questions, the answers to which might be used against them in any future criminal proceedings or might uncover further evidence against them."

Tenth Amendment

"The powers not delegated to the United States by the Constitution, nor prohibited by it to the states, are reserved to the states."

Fourteenth Amendment

". . . No State shall make or enforce any law which shall abridge the privileges or immunities of citizens of the United States; nor shall any State deprive any person of life, liberty or property, without due process of law; nor deny to any person within its jurisdiction, the equal protection of the laws."

Appellate Jurisdiction of the Supreme Court

In broad terms, to review: (1) all cases in lower federal courts, and (2) all cases in state courts in which there is involved a question of the meaning or effect of a federal statute or a constitutional provision.

Chapter 2

TENURE AND DISMISSAL

History of Tenure

The first state tenure law was passed in New Jersey in 1909.[1] A tenure law is one that—

a. Provides for continuing employment of teachers who, under its terms, have acquired permanent tenure, or continuing contract status.

b. Requires boards to comply with prescribed procedural provisions of notice, statement of charges, and right to a hearing before a tenured teacher can be dismissed or before non-renewal of the teacher's contract of employment can be effective.[2]

Before passage of such a law, many teachers were arbitrarily relieved of their positions because of political, religious, or other beliefs. Therefore, tenure is an aid in the protection of the academic freedom of the teacher and the learner.[3]

In 1873, thirty-six years before the first tenure law was passed, Charles Eliot keynoted the situation when he said "permanence of tenure is necessary to make the position of teacher one of dignity and independence." Those who confer status on teachers have been very reluctant in accepting tenure as well as adequate pay for teachers.

---

[1]DeYoung, Charles A. and Richard Wynn: *American Education*. New York: McGraw-Hill Book Company, 1960, p. 233.

[2]Wilson, Robert E.: *Education Administration*. Columbus, Ohio: Charles E. Merrill Books, Inc., 1966, p. 485.

[3]*Supra* note 1, p. 247.

Purpose of Tenure

Reasons given for tenure by the Committee on Tenure and Academic Freedom of the NEA in 1946 were the following:

1. To maintain and improve the educational opportunities of children and youth.
2. To build in the teacher that confidence and freedom which comes with a sense of stability and security as a citizen in a free republic.
3. To protect teachers in preparing children and youth for loyal, effective participation in a democratically controlled society of free men cooperating for the common welfare.
4. To enrich community life by giving permanency and continuity to the service of the teacher.
5. To encourage boards of education to place the welfare of children above the selfish interests of those political or economic groups which may seek to dominate the schools.
6. To guarantee employment conditions, providing a sense of security which will encourage teachers to attain the highest standards of professional competence.
7. To encourage the most promising young men and women to prepare for teaching as a life work, not as a stepping stone.
8. To set up definite, orderly procedures by which incompetent, unsatisfactory teachers may be dismissed.
9. To protect competent, satisfactory teachers from unjust dismissal.
10. To protect teachers in the exercise of their rights and duties as American citizens.[4]

Development of Tenure Legislation

The Committee on Tenure Legislation of the NEA compiled the following "basic principles for the development of tenure legislation," which have received the approval of many others who have devoted research to the importance of the problem:

1. Teacher tenure laws should be devised and administered

---

[4]Burnap, Percy E.: *The Teacher and the Public School System.* New York: Harper and Row, 1967, p. 404-405.

in the interest of better instruction for children.

2. Tenure laws should be accompanied by proper legal regulations governing training, certification, remuneration, and retirement allowances.

3. Tenure laws should be devised and administered as a stimulus to better preparation and more efficient service on the part of teachers.

4. Indefinite tenure should be provided after successful experience during a probationary period of adequate length, usually two or three years.

5. The right of dismissal should be in the hands of the employing board.

6. Laws establishing indefinite tenure should provide for the easy dismissal of unsatisfactory or incompetent teachers for clearly demonstrable causes, such as misconduct, incompetence, evident unfitness for teaching, persistent violation or refusal to obey laws, insubordination, neglect of duty, or malfeasance.

7. The proposed dismissal of a teacher on account of incompetence or neglect of duty should be preceded by a warning and specific statement in writing of defects.

8. In case of proposed dismissal, teachers should be granted the right of hearing.

9. Teachers who do not desire to continue in their positions should give reasonable notice in writing of their intention.

10. Suitable provision should be made for teachers already in service when putting laws into operation.

11. Indefinite tenure should be accorded to all classes of certified school employees on status of teacher, at least.[5]

Definition of Tenure

"Tenure" in its broadest sense means the duration of employment, and a teacher employed by an annual or a five-year contract has tenure in this sense for a year or for five years, as the case may be. However, the word "tenure" has developed a technical meaning in school law that refers to indefinite or permanent employment from year to year under certain conditions. Tenure

---

[5]Weber, Clarence Adams: *Personnel Problems of School Administrators.* New York: McGraw-Hill Book Company, 1954, p. 145.

in this technical sense is provided by statute; there is no common law involved. The tenure status of teachers, therefore, depends upon the provisions of the particular tenure law under which they are employed.

Tenure laws are sometimes called continuing-contract laws; continuing-contract laws are sometimes called tenure legislation. Strictly speaking, however, there are two distinct kinds of statutes regardless of interchanged terminology. A true continuing-contract law is an annual contract, or a contract for a stated period, which is automatically renewed if the teacher is not notified of nonrenewal by a specified date. Ordinarily no reasons need by given for a notice of nonrenewal, nor is any hearing required.

A tenure law, on the other hand, even if it is called a continuing-contract law, includes also certain provisions that make it definitely a tenure law. These features may be stated briefly to provide permanent status when the teacher cannot be dismissed, even at the end of a school year, except for stated causes after due notice and opportunity for self-defense.

Growth of Tenure

By 1936, there were seven states with some form of statewide tenure; fourteen states with a form of tenure in certain places for some teachers, mostly by local boards, or contracts of from one to five years; and twenty-seven states with no legislation on tenure and only annual contracts.

Figures were more than reversed by 1950. By then twenty-one states had some form of statewide tenure; twenty states had forms of tenure in certain places or contracts of from one to five years; and only seven had no legislation on tenure and only annual contracts.

In the 1950s Weber wrote that there were obstacles that needed to be resolved such as (a) some people, professional and laymen, believed teachers with tenure would not feel obligated to improve professionally any longer; (b) some people, professional and laymen, believed that incompetent, mentally ill, or physically unfit teachers "would be frozen into school systems."[6]

---

[6]*Supra* note 5, pp. 147-148.

In a study of facts concerning these obstacles, Weber found that of about 1400 teachers in summer schools in 1939, teachers with tenure attended as often as teachers without tenure. He found that in thirteen states with tenure, forty-six schools had unprecedented teacher growth. However, in seven states without tenure, only two compared with them. Another study showed twenty-one states with tenure laws had an average of 13.8 percent of teachers with a master's degree while in states with only annual contracts, only 7.6 percent earned master's degrees. More than this, he found that the average percentage of teachers teaching with less than two years of college was 9.4 percent in states with tenure. This percentage rose to sixteen percent in states without tenure. Weber concluded that tenure is conducive to teacher growth. If incompetents of any kind remain, it is not due to tenure laws but to lax enforcement of dismissal clauses.[7]

At the beginning of the 1960-61 term of school, thirty-seven states had tenure laws in effect, either statewide or in special areas only. The District of Columbia has received tenure also. Of the remaining thirteen states, five had statewide continuing-contract laws of the spring notification type. A spring notification type of continuing-contract requires a teacher to be notified in advance by a specified date that his contract will not be renewed. If he is not so notified, he is hired automatically for another year. Virginia had a law allowing local boards to automatically renew contracts if neither teacher nor board notifies the other by April 1. The other seven states provided annual or long-term contracts.[8]

Some tenure laws state that a teacher without previous tenure who has worked three out of the last five years in one district may receive tenure if he has a professional, permanent, or life certificate. Some school districts require a degree plus 27 quarter hours and three years teaching experience. A superintendent may elect to recommend one more limited contract of no more than two years, but the teacher must be given reasons with direction as to professional improvement. Unless the teacher resigns or the board has cause to terminate the contract, this continuing-contract is in effect until the age of seventy. The teacher has a right to a hearing and appeal when given required written notice by the

---

[7]*Supra* note 5, pp. 148-151.
[8]*Supra* note 2, pp. 486-487.

board that the contract is to be terminated.[9]

Types of Tenure Laws

There are two types of tenure by law or contract. This is generally misunderstood by teachers, board members, and administrators, while the public is probably ignorant about these differences. One is a contract type tenure law, which the United States Constitution prevents from being changed even though subsequent legislation is enacted because the Supreme Court has ruled one of the basic guarantees of American democracy is the "sacredness of contractual relationship." The other type is a policy stating tenure law where law sets forth a policy without contractual relation. If teachers have this type of tenure, they can lose all benefits of tenure by subsequent action of legislators because the Supreme Court has also ruled that "in matters of policy one legislature cannot tie the hands of a future legislature." In the statutes of Indiana and Illinois, it has been ruled that teachers have status by contract, whereas, in New Jersey, Oregon, California, and New York, teachers have only a policy stating law, which may be changed.[10]

In Defense of Tenure

In an article published by the Ohio Education Association, tenure was termed as "necessary" and defended strongly but in need of changes. A sixteen member panel of citizens backed by nine Ohio foundations, which make up the Commission of Public School Personnel Policies in Ohio, came to the following major conclusions as a result of this study:

> Teachers should be protected against arbitrary and unwarranted action by their employers.
>
> Professional incompetence cannot be tolerated for any reason.
>
> Tenure should not be viewed by teachers or administrators as guaranteed lifetime employment.
>
> Major changes are needed in the tenure laws.

---

[9]"Tenure: A Necessary Protection Against Arbitrary Board Action." *Ohio Schools,* XLIX, October 8, 1971, p. 14.

[10]*Supra* note 5, pp. 144-145.

School management should improve its administration of tenure.

They should be particularly protected against unfair action to terminate employment resulting from undue pressure of parents, the poor judgement of supervisors, discussion of controversial issues in their classes and their personal political actions.[11]

The Commission lay the blame for incompetent teachers retaining their positions on reluctant administrators who fear personal criticism in the defense provided for the teacher. They found in a survey of Ohio Superintendents that 93 percent claimed no termination of tenured teachers and 74 percent reported no resignation by request in the past five years, yet they reported that they do have teachers who are "patently incompetent for reasons of physical, mental, and emotional difficulties, attitudes toward children or lack of teaching ability."

In favoring changes, the Commission found that the greatest weakness is in the hearing procedure. To replace a board hearing, a three-member referee hearing was recommended without chance for a rehearing. The teacher should select one, the board another, and the third should be selected by both. Although boards should retain a final decision, it is doubtful they would refuse the decision of the referees.

The Commission favored establishment of minimum standards with time to improve before termination of a continuing-contract but disagreed that tenure was unnecessary if schools had collective bargaining.[12]

Kenneth E. Elbe, the Director of the Project to Improve College Teaching, writes that he is suspicious that the "wave of concern for tenure's adverse effects upon teaching" is due to the fact that it "protects the voicing of unpopular opinions" in a time of student protest, Vietnamization, etc. He claims that in all tenure attacks, there has been no real evidence that teaching is worse due to tenure outside of that from "documentable examples of wretched teaching, inferences can be drawn to damn the system."

Elbe points out that in the few institutions that do not use tenure there is not outstanding excellence in either their instruc-

---

[11]*Supra* note 9, pp. 13-14.
[12]*Supra* note 9, pp. 13-14.

tion or their programs. Likewise, some of the weakest institutions are those where protection is weak. On the other hand, standard-setting institutions for academic excellence are places with firm principles of tenure.

Although Elbe says he cannot prove tenure is beneficial to teaching and a small survey showed the largest number of faculty felt tenure had no good or bad effect, he gives five reasons why he thinks it is necessary in attaining excellence in teaching as well as for maintenance of freedom of inquiry:

> First, teaching that would add anything either to knowledge or wisdom must be free to explore, invent and imagine.
>
> Second, excellence in teaching grows out of trial and error, a pushing against both institutional and self-limitations.
>
> Third, an institution's excellence in teaching as in scholarship is related to its ability to hold its best people as well as to weed out its poor ones.
>
> Fourth, teaching profits from both flexibility and security. The one helps teachers break out of deadening routines; the other makes it possible for them to return with imagination and energies renewed.
>
> Fifth, excellent teaching cannot operate in a climate of fear nor be brought into being by coercion.[13]

Tenure and the Probationary Status

Practically all tenure laws require the teacher newly appointed to pass through a probationary period before acquiring tenure status. The probationary period in various states is from one to five years, most commonly three. During the probationary period, annual contracts are customary and teachers on proba-tion may be dismissed at the end of any school year. In other tenure laws, permission is given to dismiss a probationary teacher at any time during the probationary period, and in these states, the probationary teacher may be dismissed even during the school year, the annual contract having been made with the statutory limitation. Ordinarily, it is not necessary to state a reason or

[13]Eble, Kenneth E.: "Despite Attacks on Tenure, There Is No Evidence That It Actually Leads to Ineffective Teaching," *Chronicle of Higher Education*, Vol. 4, No. 29 (April 26, 1971) p. 8.

conduct a hearing before dismissing probationary teachers.

In recent years, probationary teachers have been employed under spring notification continuing-contract laws. Thus, throughout the probationary period, these teachers are automatically reemployed each ensuing year unless notified by the specified date in the spring that they will not be reemployed.

At the end of the probationary period, teachers acquire tenure status, usually by nomination of the superintendent and appointment by the school board. This procedure has allowed some abuse if the board employs a disproportionate number of probationary teachers and, by dismissing them at the end of the probationary period, prevents the majority of probationary teachers from acquiring tenure status. Probationary teachers have been dismissed and then reemployed as probationary teachers. Some laws have sought to ameliorate this practice by stating that the teacher who serves beyond the probationary period automatically acquires tenure status, or that tenure is gained at the end of the probationary period without overt sanction by the board if the teacher has not been notified of dismissal before the end of the probationary period.

Tenure by Default, Acquiescence, or Estoppel

It has been reaffirmed in New York that tenure may not be acquired by acquiescence and estoppel unless there was actual service beyond the term of probation. When a school board fails to provide notice of nonrenewal to a probationary teacher within the statutory time limit, there is a divergence of authority as to whether the teacher is entitled to any remedy and, if so, whether such remedy includes tenured status.

In a case in Tennessee[14] a notice of nonrenewal was required by April 15 of the final probationary year, but was not delivered until eleven days thereafter. Although the superintendent had notified the plaintiff teacher by letter on April 6 that his service would be needed for the following school year, the court held the superintendent's action to have no legal effect as it was not

---

[14]Snell v. Brothers, 527 S.W.2d 114 (Tenn., 1975); *Yearbook of School Law*, Topeka, Kansas: NOLPE, 1976, p. 154.

authorized by the county board of education. The court found that the teacher had completed his probationary period but that failure to send notice before the conclusion of the probationary period did not give him permanent tenure status. It did, however, result in his contract being continued for one more year. He was therefore entitled to damages for breach of that one year contract.

In Michigan, a federal district court awarded tenure to a probationary teacher when the school board failed to comply with the statute requiring not only a written notice of nonrenewal but also written notice of whether or not the teacher's performance had been satisfactory.[15] In this case, a probationary teacher had received written notice of nonrenewal but did not receive a written evaluation of his performance. By state law, absence of the latter is treated as conclusive evidence that the performance was satisfactory. The court held that the aggrieved employee was entitled to a continuing contract.

A New York court found that a probationary teacher had acquired tenure by estoppel when the school board attempted to remove him from his position.[16] The teacher's probationary period was due to end in September. Removal proceedings had been brought against him the previous year but they were not completed until October. Not until the following January, more than four months after the probationary period had expired, did the school board vote to terminate his probationary status. Since the board failed to adopt a resolution denying tenure on or before the expiration of the probationary period, the teacher acquired tenure status by estoppel.

Tenure and Dismissal

After a teacher acquires tenure status, dismissal is legal only for certain causes and certain procedures. The causes for justifiable dismissal may be enumerated in the law, or the law may be more general, stating merely that tenured teachers may be dismissed "for reasonable and just cause." Other tenure laws combine an enumeration with the general term.

---

[15]Morse v. Wozniak, 398 F. Supp. 597 (E. D. Mich., 1975).

[16]Elisofon v. Board of Education of New York City, App. Div. 2d 379, N.Y.S.2d 145 (1976); see also *Yearbook of School Law, supra* note 14, p. 155.

Before the dismissal, the tenured teacher is entitled to notice, with a statement of charges, and a hearing before the school board in which hearing the teacher may defend himself against the charges. There usually is provision for appeal from the school board's decision to dismiss, either to a higher school authority such as the state superintendent or to the courts.

A number of issues arise over the school board's procedure in dismissing teachers, regardless of the merit of the dismissal. If the school board does not follow the prescribed statutory procedure, its act in dismissing a teacher, no matter how deserved is the dismissal, may be void. Procedure in conducting the hearing is outlined in some laws with more particularity than in others. Regardless of statutory prescription, the hearing, to constitute due process, must contain certain essential features.

The teacher whose dismissal is under consideration must be given sufficient notice to prepare his self-defense before the hearing. He should be permitted to appear with counsel. The testimony of witnesses, for and against the teacher, would be taken only after the witnesses have been given an oath or affirmed that they will tell the truth. The right to subpoena witnesses should be allowed the teacher. The evidence heard in the hearing should be restricted to evidence bearing upon the charges of which the teacher has been apprised. Counsel for the teacher should have the right to present argument on the evidence and the law involved. A stenographic transcript of the hearing should be taken so that it will be available in case of an appeal.

Due process in teacher dismissals includes the following:

a. The clerk sends a written notice to the teacher of the board's intention to terminate the contract.

b. The teacher has ten days to file a written request for a hearing, which may be public or private.

c. If the teacher requests a hearing, it must be scheduled within thirty days of the request.

d. The clerk gives written notice of the hearing at least fifteen days in advance.

e. A majority of the board must conduct the hearing.

f. The board must provide a record of the hearing to the teacher.

g. Both parties must be represented by counsel.

h. Witnesses may be required to testify within limitations.

i. The board by a majority vote may terminate the contract.
j. If the teacher is rehired, the record is erased and back pay is given.
k. The teacher, if fired, may appeal to the court of common pleas within thirty days after the receipt of the termination notice.

Tenure laws, being an abrogation of the freedom of contract, a common law privilege, are sometimes construed by the courts strictly, because they make a change in the common law.

Tenure provisions, state or local, provide for teachers a legislative or a contract status, depending on how the law is written. If the teacher has a legislative status, his employment depends entirely on the legislative enactment; if the legislature changes the law, the status of the teacher changes. Thus a teacher on tenure may lose his tenure status if the tenure law is repealed, if it has established legislative status for him. However, if the teacher has a contract status under the tenure law, his employment, although depending partly on the statute, depends also upon the contractual relation created by the statute. Under such circumstances if the legislature changes the tenure law, it does not apply to those teachers who have already acquired tenure because the Federal Constitution forbids the impairment of the obligation of contracts. The change in a tenure law of this type applies only to teachers subsequently employed or those in a probationary status.

Types of Tenure Laws

The distinction between a contract-type tenure law and a policy stating legislative tenure law is not always clear. There are several laws that include a reservation of the right to amend or repeal, obviously creating only a legislative status in which no vested rights may accrue. In these states there could be no judicial determination that the law established a contractual status. However, most tenure laws do not contain this reservation, and the question is one that must be decided by the courts. In many states, the issue has not come before the courts. Indiana has a judicially designated contract type tenure law. Where the issue has arisen in other states, their tenure laws have been held to be policy stating legislation.

A policy stating tenure law is just as good as a contract type tenure law, until the legislature changes the policy in a way as to show an intention to deprive tenured teachers of their rights acquired under the previous provisions. In Wisconsin the law was repealed; in several states it has been amended so as to repeal its application to certain kinds of teachers, usually rural or aged teachers.

Reasons for Dismissal

School boards are authorized to dismiss a permanent tenure teacher by provisions in tenure laws, many of which include dismissal for personal reasons, such as immorality. Probationary teachers in tenure districts may be dismissed if they do not achieve the standards set by school boards and administrators, standards of personal conduct as well as professional. So also, teachers under contract for a specified term may be dismissed before the termination of the contract without liability for breach of contract on the part of the school board if certain charges can be upheld by sufficient evidence. Teaching certificates can be revoked. Applications for teaching certificates can be denied. Applications for teaching positions can be refused.

By any of these methods, a teacher may be excluded from the profession for which he was trained, upon charges of immorality, conduct unbecoming a teacher, dishonesty, intemperance, mental derangement, inefficiency, incompetency, etc. (*see* Fig. 1)

Dismissal of Teachers

The following principles are taken from *School in the Legal Structure.*

1. A school board's power to dismiss a teacher may be derived from statute, or in the absence of statute, it may stem from an implied authority to dismiss for adequate cause.
2. The power to dismiss for just cause is absolute and may not be limited by contract.
3. A teacher (as a general rule) may not be dismissed without a justifiable cause before the expiration of a contract.
4. Where the method of dismissal is prescribed by statute,

Figure 1

STATUTORY GROUNDS FOR THE DISMISSAL OR SUSPENSION OF TEACHERS

	Other	Failure to Obey State Laws	Cause (Good, Just, Sufficient)	Incompetency	Unfitness for Service	Negligence - Neglect of Duty	Failure to Provide Designated Instruction	Failure to Attend Required Institutes	Inefficiency	Insubordination	Refusal to Obey Regulations	Noncompliance with School Laws	Disloyalty, Subversive Act	Contract Violation, Cancellation, Annulment, Breach	Conviction of Specified Crime	Immorality	Untruthfulness, Dishonesty, Falsification of Application Records	Drunkenness, Intemperance	Addiction to Drugs and/or Selling Drugs	Cruelty	Conduct Unbecoming a Teacher, Misconduct in Office	Unprofessional Conduct	Violation of Code of Ethics	Revocation of Certificate	Incapacity
Alabama			X	X		X	X			X						X									
Alaska			X									X				X									
Arizona	X																								
Arkansas														X											
California	X			X							X				X	X	X	X				X		X	
Colorado			X	X		X	X			X				X		X									
Connecticut			X	X					X	X						X									
Delaware			X		X					X			X			X					X				
Florida			X		X					X					X	X				X	X				
Georgia																									
Hawaii			X			X			X	X	X					X									
Idaho	X														X						X				
Illinois			X	X	X											X						X			
Indiana			X	X	X						X	X				X									
Iowa			X	X	X																				
Kansas	X		X	X						X	X	X				X					X				
Kentucky			X		X					X	X					X					X				
Louisiana	X		X		X										X										
Maine																									
Maryland			X		X					X						X					X				
Massachusetts			X							X	X	X	X		X						X				X
Michigan												X						X							
Minnesota			X		X					X	X		X	X	X	X					X				
Mississippi			X	X	X									X		X			X		X				
Missouri	X		X		X					X	X	X	X	X		X									
Montana				X	X					X		X				X									

	Other	Failure to Obey State Laws	Cause (Good, Just, Sufficient)	Incompetency	Unfitness for Service	Negligence - Neglect of Duty	Failure to Provide Designated Instruction	Failure to Attend Required Institutes	Inefficiency	Insubordination	Refusal to Obey Regulations	Noncompliance with School Laws	Disloyalty, Subversive Act	Contract Violation, Cancellation, Annulment, Breach	Conviction of Specified Crime	Immorality	Untruthfulness, Dishonesty, Falsification of Application Records	Drunkenness, Intemperance	Addiction to Drugs and/or Selling Drugs	Cruelty	Conduct Unbecoming a Teacher, Misconduct in Office	Unprofessional Conduct	Violation of Code of Ethics	Revocation of Certificate	Incapacity
Nebraska	X	X		X		X				X		X													
Nevada																									
New Hampshire				X												X		X							
New Jersey			X						X	X															
New Mexico			X																						
New York				X		X			X		X					X							X		
North Carolina		X	X	X		X			X		X	X			X	X		X							X
North Dakota			X											X											
Ohio			X						X		X					X									
Oklahoma				X	X							X				X					X				
Oregon																									
Pennsylvania				X	X							X				X				X	X				
Rhode Island			X									X													
South Carolina			X																						
South Dakota																									
Tennessee			X		X	X			X	X	X		X		X	X		X	X	X		X	X	X	
Texas																									
Utah																									
Vermont				X		X					X			X							X				
Virginia		X	X		X				X	X	X					X									
Washington																									
West Virginia				X	X						X			X		X					X	X	X		
Wisconsin			X			X					X					X									
Wyoming		X	X		X					X						X									

such method must be followed in order for the dismissal to be valid.

5. Even though no method of procedure is set out, the teacher is entitled to notices of charges against him and to a fair hearing before an impartial board.

6. As a general rule, a removal for a cause not authorized by statute or contract and outside the discretionary powers of the school authorities are invalid.

7. The burden of proof rests upon the school board in proving incompetency, because the teacher's certificate is *prima facie* evidence of competency.

8. The teacher has the right to have competency determined on the basis of service.

9. The board can demand of teachers only average qualifications, not the highest, in determining incompetency.

10. The teacher may seek redress in the court if he feels that the evidence presented by the board is not sufficient to establish his incompetency and if he has exhausted all administrative remedies prior to this.

11. The courts are inclined to accept the testimony of superintendents, supervisors, and principals as the teacher's ability to perform his duties.

12. Where school board's action appears to be for the welfare of the children, the dismissal of a teacher is likely to win judicial approval.[17]

State statutes vary in stipulating the causes for dismissal of teachers.

Dismissal for Cause

A large number of cases have been filed by teachers protesting dismissal for a variety of acts that they have argued should not be considered as "just cause." While "cause" is a statutory ground for teachers' suspension and dismissal, it is often used as a miscellaneous category. Very seldom do "just cause" terminations directly relate to the teacher's performance or level of preparation, but to certain aspects of their personal life—

---

[17]Bolmeier, Edward C.: *The School In The Legal Structure.* Cincinnati, Ohio: The W.H. Anderson Company, 1973, p. 194. Also see various issues of *American Jurisprudence* and *Corpus Juris Secundum.*

especially their sexual behavior when school administrators or boards have found it to be offensive to the moral standards of the community.

Incompetency

Dismissals for incompetency can take on the character of a disciplinary action. This is especially true in situations in which the teacher refuses to take steps to improve his classroom performance. It has been upheld by the courts that "School boards can demand of teachers only average qualifications, not the highest, in determining incompetency."[18] Also, school boards may use the grounds of incompetency to justify the dismissal not only for ineffective job performance but also a variety of behaviors that may be related only indirectly to the employee's duties.[19]

Incompetency is defined almost universally by different sources. For example, Funk and Wagnall's Standard Dictionary defines it as "General lack of capacity of fitness, or lack of the special qualities required for a particular purpose." Webster's New International Dictionary defines it as "Want of physical, intellectual, or moral ability; insufficiency; inadequacy; specifically, want of legal qualifications of fitness." Black's Law Dictionary defines it as "Lack of ability or fitness to discharge the required duty."

In nonrenewal actions, unless there is a statutory requirement to do so, the school board may decide whether or not to give reasons.

State statutes frequently require the notice of deficiencies and the time period for correcting them before a teacher may be dismissed for incompetency. Failure to adhere to the statutory requirements is most likely to invalidate the dismissal. For example, when two Alaska probationary teachers were dismissed at midterm for incompetency, it was ruled that a failure to provide a hearing violated their Fourteenth Amendment rights.[20]

---

[18]Bolmeier, *supra* note 17, p. 194.
[19]Delon, Floyd G.: *Legal Controls on Teacher Conduct: Teacher Discipline.* Topeka, Kansas: NOLPE Monograph Series, 1977, p. 29.
[20]Nicholas v. Echert, 504 P.2d 1359 (Alaska, 1973).

Although the state statutes do not require a hearing, the court ruled that the stigma resulting from dismissal during the term of the contract sufficiently overrode the lack of such statutory provisions.

Under the common law and under the statutes generally, incompetency constitutes a valid cause for dismissal of a teacher.

A teacher, it has been held, is guilty of incompetency when he so conducts himself as to forfeit the good will and respect of the community. In a Pennsylvania case, a teacher acted as a waitress, and on occasion a bartender, in her husband's beer garden after school hours and during the summer. In the presence of pupils she took a drink of beer, shook dice with customers for drinks, and played and showed the customers how to play a pinball machine. The court sustained her dismissal for incompetence.[21]

Poor teaching is usually construed to mean incompetency or inefficiency in a legal sense. For example, a tenured teacher who taught in the Cleveland public schools for twenty-seven years was terminated for poor teaching (incompetency).[22] Inability to maintain discipline is commonly considered as incompetency warranting dismissal.[23]

Unprofessional Conduct

"Unprofessional conduct" or "conduct unbecoming a teacher" is a very vague ground for dismissal because there are no absolute standards of teacher conduct. While this charge is often included with other charges, conduct unbecoming a teacher is occasionally the single justification used.[24] (The statute of only one state distinguishes between "conduct unbecoming a teacher" and "unprofessional conduct.")

Six Boston teachers were dismissed for conduct unbecoming a teacher and their dismissals were affirmed by the courts.[25] This case centered on how much community participation should be allowed in the school. The parents became angry because of the

---

[21]Horosko v. School District of Mt. Pleasant, 335 Pa. 369, 6 Atl.2d 866.
[22]Applebaum v. Wulff, 42 Ohio ops 434, 58 Ohio Lavs, 260, 95 N.E.2d (1950).
[23]Guthrie v. Board of Education of Jefferson County, 298 S.W.2d 691 (Ky. 1957).
[24]*Supra* note 19, p. 40.
[25]Decanio v. School Committee of Boston, 260 N.E.2d 767 (Mass., 1970).

limits placed on community participation, thereby taking their children home and causing school to be closed for the day.

"The six plaintiffs without seeking permission of their superiors accompanied the demonstrators and children to Shaw House (a liberation school) and conducted classes for the entire day."[26]

The next day the teachers were suspended and later dismissed. A subsequent appeal was dismissed.

Immorality

The term "immorality" varies with time and place. Immorality is not limited to sexual misbehavior. The Pennsylvania Supreme Court has ruled:

> Immorality is not essentially confined to a deviation from sex morality; it may be such a course of conduct as offends the morals of the community, and is a bad example to the youth whose ideals a teacher is supposed to foster and elevate.[27]

A California teacher brought action to compel the state board of education to restore his teaching credentials.[28] The revocation by the board was response to charges of immoral and unprofessional conduct alleging "that at a public beach the teacher had rubbed, touched and fondled the private sexual parts" of another man.[29] In his testimony the teacher acknowledged a past history of homosexual behavior. In affirming the trial court's decision supporting the action of the board of education, the appelate court said:

> In view of the appelant's statutory duty as a teacher to "endeavor to impress on the minds of the pupils the principles of morality" and his necessarily close association with children in the discharge of his professional duties as teacher, there is in our minds an obvious rational connection between his homosexual conduct on the beach and the consequent action of the respondent in revoking his certificate.[30]

---

[26]Decanio v. School Committee of Boston, 410 U.S. 929 (1971).

[27]Horosko v. Mt. Pleasant Township School District, 6 A2d 866 (Pa., 1939).

[28]Sarac v. State Board of Education, 249 Cal. App.2d 58, 57 Cal. Rptr. 69 (1972).

[29]Sarac v. State Board of Education, 249 Cal. App.2d 60, 57 Cal. Rptr. 71 (1972).

[30]Sarac v. State Board of Education, 249 Cal. App.2d 63, 57 Cal. Reptr. 72-73 (1972).

The Eighth Circuit Court found that a school board in a small community was justified in dismissing a single female teacher who persisted in living with a male friend while not married. The teacher's classroom performance was satisfactory in every way. The court considered particularly important the smallness of the community and the fact that the teacher's behavior would have an adverse effect on the young school-age children.[31]

A pregnant, unwed teacher on probationary status may constitutionally be denied reemployment because of her pregnancy, since there is a rational relationship between the out-of-wedlock pregnancy and the board's interest in conserving marital values.[32]

A male teacher who entered a girls' bathroom, seized a female student from therein, and characterized her as a whore, was held not to be immoral.[33]

Unfitness to Teach

The specific charge in a number of recent dismissal actions has been "unfitness" to teach. Conduct that provides sufficient evidence of the teacher's unfitness is generally serious enough to justify revoking the certificate as well as terminating the contract. Charges such as "grave lack of judgment," conviction of a felony, or any crime involving "moral turpitude" are used.

The Iowa Supreme Court considered a revocation action for immorality based on adultery.[34] The plaintiff was an art teacher/coach who had an affair with a married home economics teacher. They were subsequently caught in the back seat of a car partially clothed on a country road by the husband and friends. The male teacher offered to resign his postion, but the school board refused to accept his resignation. The state board instituted revocation proceedings and cancellation of his certificate in spite of strong support for the teacher from the pupils, teachers, administrators, and the community. The trial court sustained the action, whereby the defendent appealed to the Supreme Court. The Supreme

---

[31]Sullivan v. Meade Independent School District No. 101, 530 F.2d 799 (8th Cir., 1976). Also *Yearbook of School Law.* Topeka, Kansas: NOLPE, 1977, p. 171.

[32]Brown v. Bathke, 416 F. Supp. 1194 (D. Neb., 1976).

[33]Thompson v. Wake City Board of Education, 230 S.E.2d 164 (N.C. App., 1976).

[34]Erb v. Iowa State Board of Public Instruction, 216 N.W.2d 339 (Iowa, 1974).

Court upheld the ruling by the school board for revocation and cancellation of his certificate.

Neglect of Duty

Under the common law and under statutes providing for the dismissal of teachers for neglect of duty, the courts have been called upon in a number of cases to determine what constitutes neglect within the contemplation of the law. Frequent tardiness has been held a justifiable grounds for dismissal.[35]

Temporary absence from school without sufficient cause likewise constitutes that degree of neglect that justifies a school board in dismissing a teacher. It has been held, however, that delay in reporting to duty at the beginning of the school year is not such neglect of duty as to warrant the dismissal of a teacher. Thus, in a Colorado case[36] it was held that a delay in reporting from September 6 to September 28 did not terminate a teacher's contract.

In another case, a black principal in Georgia claimed his dismissal resulted from racial bias.[37] The evidence presented indicated that he failed to hold fire drills, to secure the building, to attend certain school meetings, to cooperate in giving achievement tests, and to follow school regulations on the use of state adopted textbooks. The court accepted this evidence as sufficient grounds for dismissal.

Insubordination

Insubordination consists of the "unwillingness to submit to authority." Insubordination has become the most frequently cited reason for removing errant teachers.

The term "insubordination" is not defined in the statutes, but unquestionably it includes the willful refusal of a teacher to obey the reasonable rules and regulations of his employing board of education.[38]

---

[35]School Directors of District No. 1. Birch, 93 Ill. App. 499.
[36]School District No. 1 v. Parker, 206 PAC (Colo.) 521.
[37]Glover v. Daniel, 318 F. Supp. 1070 (N.D. Ga., 1969).
[38]State v. Board of Education of Fairfield, 252 Ala. 695 of S.2d 689 (1949).

The refusal of a teacher to attend an "open house," where parents had the opportunity to visit school and to confer with teachers regarding the work of the children, was construed by the court to be an act of insubordination. In commenting on the case,[39] the court stated its belief in the following statement:

> Any school teacher who lacks an understanding of her responsibility to be present on this occasion and who arrogantly refuses to obey the direction of her employer to be there and instead follows her own special whims and pleasures can properly be held by the board to be unfit to continue in the employment of that board. The plaintiff here has demonstrated a lack of respect for "the glorious tradition of the teaching profession."[40]

In *Ahern v. Board of Education of Grandview*, the courts rejected a Nebraska teacher's request for injunctive relief under the Civil Rights Act.[41] The teacher's unorthodox teaching style and her outspokenness resulted in warning from the school administrators. The incident leading to her discharge occurred when she returned to duty after an absence and reacted to a report about problems between a substitute teacher and her students. The plaintiff said to her class, "That bitch! I hope that if this happens again . . . all of you walk out."[42] In regard to the teacher's statement in the classroom, the court said:

> I am persuaded that the exercising of a constitutional right was not the reason for the discharge. Although a teacher has a right to express opinions and concerns, as does any other citizen on matters of public concern, by virtue of the First and Fourteenth Amendments . . . I doubt that she has the right to express them during class in deliberate violation of a superior's admonition not to do so, when the subject of her opinions and concerns is directly related to students and teacher discipline.[43]

Failure to Observe School Board Regulations

A public school teacher is bound to obey all reasonable

---

[39] Johnson v. U.S. District Joint School Board, 201 Pa. Supp. 375, 191 A.2d 897 (1963).
[40] Johnson v. U.S. District Joint School Board, 201 Pa. Supp. 375, 191 A.2d 900 (1963).
[41] 327 F. Supp. 1391 (D. Nebr., 1971).
[42] 327 F. Supp. 1393 (D. Nebr., 1971).
[43] 327 F. Supp. 1393 (D. Nebr., 1971).

regulations of the board that employs him,[44] it makes no difference whether the rules were in force at the date of his employment or were promulgated at a later date.[45] Rules governing the relations of a board with its teachers in force at the time of employment are, by implication, read into the contract.[46] All contracts are made in contemplation of the law, and a teacher implies consent to obey all rules a board may legally make.[47]

Remedies for Dismissed Teachers

A teacher who has been illegally dismissed has a right of action against the school board in its corporate capacity for breach of contract;[48] there is no right of action against the school board members personally unless they have acted maliciously or in bad faith.[49] A teacher who is wrongfully discharged may bring action for damages.[50] Two types of damages may be awarded by the courts—reinstatement or back pay. In a case involving the wrongful termination of a nontenured teacher, the courts held that while an award of back pay or damages will be granted, reinstatement is not required in every case of wrongful termination. In one case, a probationary teacher[51] was found to have been wrongfully terminated and her "liberty" interest violated by being terminated for "persistent insubordination" without procedural due process and without any basis in fact for the charge.[52] In this case, the appropriate remedy was not reinstatement but a hearing to give her an opportunity to clear her name, and damages for any injury between the time of discharge and the time when the burden on her right to pursue her teaching career had been lifted. The board was required to consider the teacher for reemployment and to pay damages for breach of contract.

---

[44]Board of Education v. Swan, 250 Pac.2d (Calif.); Leddy v. Board of Education, 160 Ill. App. 187.

[45]Farrell v. Board of Education, 122 N.Y.S. 289.

[46]McLellan v. Board of St. Louis Public Schools, 15 Mo. App. 362.

[47]School District of Dennison Township v. Padden, 89 Pa St. 395.

[48]Underwood v. Board of County School Commissioners, 103 Md. 181, 63 Atl. 221.

[49]Gregory v. Small, 39 Ohio St. 346; Burton v. Fulton, 49 Pa. St. 151.

[50]Sarle v. School District No. 27, 255 Pac (Ariz.) 994.

[51]*Yearbook of School Law, supra* note 14, p. 196.

[52]Morris v. Board of Education of Laurel School District 401 F. Supp. 188 (D.Del., 1975); also *Yearbook of School Law, supra* note 14, p. 196.

In another case, a probationary teacher was wrongfully terminated for being a practicing homosexual. She was awarded monetary damages for the remainder of her contract and for an additional half year, but the court denied reinstatement on the grounds that reinstatement was a discretionary remedy and was not warranted given the personal animosities and controversy surrounding the entire situation.[53] The court declared that reinstatement was an "extraordinarily equitable remedy,"[54] limited to teacher dismissals involving racial discrimination and reprisals for the exercise of free speech.[55]

The general rules of contract law that award back pay are reduced by the amount of money actually earned that would not otherwise have been earned to school employees.[56] The burden of proof as to the availability of alternative employment and failure to mitigate damages rests with the school district.

The general rule is that attorney's fees are not recoverable by an employee who successfully contests an improper action of the school board.[57] However, attorney's fees are recoverable where expressly provided for by statute. When attorney's fees are recoverable, the amount is based on such factors as the hourly rate in the area and the number of hours devoted to the successful portions of the litigation.

Summary

The purpose of the Tenure Act was to maintain an adequate and competent teaching staff, free from political and personal arbitrary influence, whereby capable and competent teachers might feel secure and more efficiently perform their duty of instruction, but it was not the intention of the legislature to confer any special privileges or immunities upon professional employees to retain permanently their position and pay regardless of a place to work and pupils to be taught; neither was it the

---

[53]Burton v. Cascade School District, Union High School, 512 F.2d 850 (9th Cir., 1975); see *Yearbook of School Law, supra* note 14, p. 197.

[54]Burton v. Cascade School District, Union High School, 512 F.2d 853 (9th Cir., 1975).

[55]*Yearbook of School Law, supra* note 14, p. 197.

[56]*Yearbook of School Law, supra* note 14, p. 200.

[57]Alyeska Pipeline Co. v. Wilderness Society, 421 U.S. 240, 247 (1975); see *Yearbook of School Law, supra* note 14, p. 201.

intention of the legislature to have the Tenure Act interfere with the control of school policy and the courses of study selected by the administrative bodies.

Teacher tenure status is not intended to guarantee teachers the right to teach at any particular schools; they do not prevent a school board from assigning teachers to the various positions in the school system. That is, a school board may make any reasonable reassignment, but the work assigned must be of the same grade and rank as that teacher had when he acquired tenure status.

Tenure statutes do not prevent boards of education from making any reasonable changes in teachers' salaries. There must be no discrimination as between individual teachers, but a school board can change its salary schedules as policy may from time to time dictate.

Chapter 3

CONTRACT OF EMPLOYMENT; CERTIFICATION

The employment of public school teachers and other professional employees is accomplished by agreements entered into between the governing bodies of schools commonly referred to as local boards of education. These agreements or employment contracts, as a general rule, are also the points of reference for determining the rights and responsibilities of educational personnel. In addition to the terms and conditions expressly provided in the employment contract, other conditions or requirements may be imposed by relevant statutes that are incorporated into the employment contract by operation of law.

In practically every state, there is some legislation regarding the employment of teachers. In many nontenure areas, legislation provides the length of contract by which teachers may be employed, the procedure to be followed, and often the causes to be considered justifiable reasons for dismissal.

Definition of Contracts

Any contract for a specified length of time is a term contract. A contract is an agreement enforceable by law. The word "contract" is used for the agreement as well as for the document that is evidence of the agreement. A contract usually need not be in writing to be enforceable unless so prescribed by statute. Many school laws require written contracts for the employment of teachers, and in a few states the contract form is prescribed. In those states, an agreement that is oral, or on a form other than the one required, is not enforceable by law.

A contract must be certain and definite stating the service sought and the salary to be paid. The contract becomes binding when it is accepted. Acceptance must be unequivocal and in compliance with the terms of the offer. In general, acceptance may be a simple assent as well as by signing a document, but when stipulated by law, teachers' contracts of employment must be in writing.

Types of Contracts

Teachers are employed under three types of contracts: (1) term contracts, (2) continuing contracts, and (3) tenure contracts. A term contract (in some school districts it is referred to as a limited contract) is issued normally for the current school year. In other districts, a limited contract is issued for a term not to exceed five years to teachers holding temporary or provisional certificates or those who hold professional or higher certificates but who are not eligible for a continuing or tenure contract.

Under Ohio law when a limited contract expires and a teacher is not eligible for a continuing (tenure) contract, a local school board may: (1) grant continuing status; (2) grant one more limited contract of either one or two years duration and provide reasons directed toward professional development; (3) not re-employ.

A continuing contract (in some districts referred to as tenure contracts) remains in effect until a teacher dies, resigns, voluntarily retires, is retired by board actions, or is suspended or terminated for cause. In districts that view continuing as different from tenure contracts, continuing contracts are those teaching contracts that, if not terminated by either party by certain procedures (usually notice by April 30), continue on a year-to-year basis. Under the above definition, in some states, no reason for termination is required, and the board's compliance with the requisite notice provisions leaves the teacher with no recourse.

To become eligible for a tenured contract, in some districts, a teacher must have taught 27 consecutive months and acquired 18 semester and/or 27 quarter hours above the basic degree. Some districts require a master's degree. The requirements are not uniform from state to state.

Elements of Contracts

Both parties to a contract must have the legal capacity to enter into an agreement. Some contracts are unenforceable because they were executed without due regard for proper procedure. In general, the elements of a contract are (1) mutual assent (that is, offer and acceptance); (2) compensation; (3) legally competent parties; (4) subject matter not prohibited by law; (5) agreement in form required by law.[1]

Mutual assent means in effect that there must be a "meeting of the minds." The parties (board of education and the party involved) must agree as to the subject covered, amount of remuneration, time of performance, and other details.

Compensation is the amount of remuneration each party pays for the promise or performance of the other. Some compensation must be present to constitute a valid contract. To be legally binding, a contract cannot require one party to do all the giving without requiring something of adequate value in return. Compensation may be: (1) money; (2) goods; (3) services; or (4) something of value.

Legally competent parties means both parties must have legal capacity to enter into an agreement. The contract must be one into which the board of education has the legal power to enter, and the other party must be empowered to bind himself or his corporation. Contracts beyond the power of the board, called *ultra vires*, are not enforceable.[2]

Ratification

If a contract is defectively executed and therefore voidable, it may be turned into a binding agreement by ratification; if the contract is ruled void, however, it cannot be ratified. Ratification of a defective and voidable contract may be accomplished by subsequent action by a board of education when it follows the proper procedures.

A voidable contract is considered ratified if a board accepts

---

[1] Reutter, E. Edmund, Jr. and Robert R. Hamilton: *The Law of Public Education.* Mineola, New York: The Foundation Press, 1976, p. 318.

[2] *Supra* note 1.

partial performance or less than was originally stipulated. A contract that is void because of the legal disability of one of the parties cannot be ratified (even by subsequent action by the board); however, one which is voidable because of defective procedure can be ratified even by acceptance of partial performance.

Ratification of a contract renders it as valid as if it had been made in accordance with law or in a legal frame. While there are a few cases to the contrary, it is usually held that there can be no partial ratification of a contract. The contract must be ratified as a whole or not at all.

1. Ratification may be either expressed or implied.
2. Ratification must be unequivocal—done in compliance with the law relative to the original contract.
3. Ratification must be done with full knowledge—district accepts and retains the benefits of the contract.
4. When a qualified teacher whose contract is invalid is allowed to teach and is paid for his services, the contract has been ratified.
5. Once ratified, a contract is just as legal and binding as if it was proper in the first place.
6. The entire contract must be ratified.

Ultra Vires Contracts

A school district cannot be held liable for contracts that are beyond its power to make. The courts have ruled that one who enters into a contract is obligated to inform himself on whether the school district has the authority to make the contract in question. The power of school districts is a matter of public records. Those who contract with a school district do so at their own peril. For instance, contracting parties may recover equipment and other materials only if it can be done without damage to the building or installations.

Void Contracts

Contracts that are void cannot be ratified. Contracts that have been ruled void are:

1.   An oral contract where state law requires that the particular contract be in writing.[3]
2.   Contracts with teachers without certificates.[4]
3.   Contracts that exceed the amount that a district is permitted to spend in one year.
4.   Contracts in which condition precedents have not been met, such as the requirement that all teachers be recommended by the superintendent.

Contracts of this type cannot be ratified, nor can persons be paid for services rendered, even if the board is willing to pay for the service.

Voidable Contracts

Voidable contracts are those containing all of the essential elements of a contract but at the same time embracing some irregularity that permits a party to take action to have it set aside. The irregularlity is often correctable. The courts have held the following to be voidable:[5]

1.   Contracts entered into with prospective teachers who at the time of contract did not hold a license but later secured one.[6]
2.   Contracts with individual board members of the school board and not the board itself.[7]
3.   Employment of a teacher at a meeting not attended by a majority of board members.[8]
4.   Employment of a teacher by the superintendent, i.e. the superintendent did not recommend the candidate to the board but extended the contract.[9]

Rights and Responsibilities after Employment

In the absence of a statute providing otherwise, the rights and

---

[3]Leland v. School District No. 28, 80 N.W. 354 (Minn. 1899).
[4]Perkins v. Inhabitants of Town Standish, 62 A.2d 321 (Me., 1948).
[5]Peterson, LeRoy J., Richard A. Rossmiller, and Malin M. Volz: *The Law and Public School Operation.* New York: Harper and Row, 1969, p. 91.
[6]Jennes v. School District No. 31, 12 Minn. 377 (1867).
[7]Smith v. School District No. 57, 42 Atl. 368 (Pa., 1898).
[8]School District No. 39 v. Shelton, 109 Pac. 67 (Okla., 1910).
[9]State *ex rel.* Kenny v. Jones, 224 S.W. 1041 (Tenn., 1920).

responsibilities of the parties to an employment contract are determined by the express or implied terms of the contract. Almost all states have some type of legislation relating to the contracts of public school teachers. To the extent that they are relevant, these statutes are uniformly held to be part of teachers' contracts whether or not they are expressly incorporated therein.

As a general rule, the reasonable rules and regulations of a school board are also held to be a part of the teachers' contracts: it has been held that a teacher's failure or refusal to comply with such rules and regulations is cause for dismissal even though the evidence showed that the teacher was not aware of the rule or regulation. To meet the legal requirements of a written contract, it is not necessary that all rules and regulations be contained in the formal written document. Terms may be found in (1) letters of transmittal, (2) minutes of board meetings, or (3) board policy ˹manual.

Dismissal Procedures

The board's power to appoint teachers carries the implied power to dismiss, subject to the restrictions provided by law.[10] Most states require the board to give proper notice of their intentions not to renew a contract. The notice must comply with state laws. The wording of the notice must be explicit in order to clearly convey its meaning. If the notice is ambiguous or obscure, it is insufficient and can be disregarded. In other words, the notice must sufficiently inform the person of the board's intent not to renew a contract.

In addition to the requirement that the notice be clearly stated, there is a minimum time period within which the notice must be received. When the notice is not received within the proper time limit, the notice is generally void, and a teacher is entitled to a contract. If the law states a person is to receive such notice on April 30, then that is the final date. If the board should send the notice later than that date, or send it on April 30, and one receives it the following day, then the person is entitled to a contract.

There is a definite form and procedure that must be followed in

---

[10]Hazard, William R.: *Education and the Law: Cases and Materials on Public Schools.* New York: The Free Press, 1971, p. 280.

notifying a person of the board's intent not to renew a contract. If the law says written notice, oral notice is not valid. If the law stipulates the notice must be sent by registered or certified mail to the teacher's last known address, placing the letter in a teacher's mailbox at school is not sufficient.

The following cases are cited to emphasize the above point. The Supreme Court of Alabama decided that notice of nonrenewal sent to a nontenured teacher at a wrong address did not fulfill statutory requirements even though the teacher discovered a carbon in his personnel file shortly after the relevant date. The evidence was deemed insufficient to show actual notice and the case was remanded.[11]

A court in Massachusetts overturned a trial courts determination that a nonrenewal principal, who had abundant actual notice that he would not be renewed, had not attempted to avoid statutory notice when his wife refused to wake him to receive a registered letter and "forgot" to bring it to his attention until after the statutory notice period.[12]

Resignation and Abandonment of Contract

Closely allied to the dismissal of teachers, regulated by tenure laws or principles of contract law, is the problem of the resignation of teachers. If the school board is required to give teachers due notice before dismissal, teachers should give notice to the school board of their intention to quit the job, and should not leave at a moment's notice. Many contracts provide for the withholding of the salary due, or a stated sum, if the teacher quits before the end of the school term for which he is employed.

If a teacher resigns and the resignation is accepted, the teacher cannot thereafter change his mind and claim the position. A teacher may rescind his resignation if he does so before the board has acted upon it. When a group of teachers go on strike, they are abandoning their contracts. If employed by a term contract, striking teachers have breached their contracts; if in tenure status, they have, theoretically at least, abandoned their tenure status. A school board could require teachers who had tenure status prior to the strike to fulfill the probationary period anew.

---

[11]Strickland v. Berger, 336 So. 2d 176 (Ala. Sup. Ct., 1976).
[12]Conte v. School Community of Methuen, 356 N.E.2d 261 (Mass. App., 1976).

Termination of a Contract

Under the general principles of contract law, a school board as an employer has no legal right to terminate a teacher's contract by dismissal before the end of the contract period except for a cause that amounts to a material breach of contract on the part of the teacher.

A teacher who has been dismissed without sufficient justification or cause may recover damages in suit for breach of contract. In determining the amount of damages, the general contract rule is that an employee who has been wrongfully dismissed may recover the total amount that would have been received under the employment contract if it had not been breached, less any sum which a person has earned or could have earned by reasonable effort in other suitable and similar employment for which the person is qualified.

Certification

The state has plenary power with respect to teachers' certificates. A teacher's certificate is not a property right, and it has none of the elements of a contract between a teacher and the state. The certificate is a document indicating that the holder has met the legal requirements to follow the teaching profession.

Holding a teaching certificate does not by itself give the holder the right to demand a position except in rare instances. A certificate is a mere privilege conferred by the state and is held subject to any law in force at the time of its issuance or any future law providing for its forfeiture.[13] The state reserves the right to impose new and additional burdens upon the holder of a certificate. A certificate to teach in the public schools is merely a license granted by the state and is revocable by the state at its pleasure.

Local boards may require qualifications in addition to those mandated by the state for certification.[14] They may add any qualifications that are reasonably related to performance in the position and that is not barred by constitutional or statutory considerations.

---

[13]Stone v. Fritts, 169 Ind. 361, 82 N.E. 792, 15 L.R.A. (N.S.) 1147, 14 Ann. Cas. 295.
[14]Board of Education for Montgomery Co. v. Messer, 257 Ky. 836, 79 S.W.2d 224 (1935).

Certification laws typically include general and specific requirements. The general requirements usually include such factors as age, good moral character, citizenship, and adequate physical condition. Eighteen is considered the minimum age for acquisition of a certificate. In some states an exception is made in the requirement that a person must be a citizen in order to be awarded a certificate. For example, those teaching foreign languages or on exchange from a foreign country may be issued a conditional certificate. For others, declaration of intent to become a citizen will suffice under a few laws, but if such persons do not follow through and become an American citizen within a specified time limit, the conditionally granted certificate is revoked. Specific requirements differentiate the training for various teaching levels (elementary or secondary) and teaching fields (science, history, home economics, etc.).

The state department of education or any agency therein is usually made the exclusive certifying authority in the state, and the certificates it issues are valid throughout the entire state. In this regard, the state department of education or the designated certifying agent therein is the only one who may revoke a certificate or grant a certificate (see Fig. 2).

Revocation

When a statute authorizes revocation of certificates for certain enumerated causes, a certificate cannot be revoked for any cause other than those specified.[15] The statutes of most states provide for revocation and suspension of certificates by the issuing authority. Alabama law contains a statute that allows the state superintendent of education to revoke a certificate. The Alabama statute reads:

> The state superintendent of education shall have the authority to revoke any certificate issued under the provisions of this chapter when the holder has been guilty of immoral conduct or indecent behavior.[16]

There are approximately twenty-five stated legal causes or grounds for the dismissal or suspension of teachers (these

---

[15]Stone v. Fritts, 169 Ind. 361, 82 N.E. 792, 15 L.R.A. (N.S.) 1147, 14 Ann. Cas. 295.
[16]See O.R.S. 342. 175; also, *Substantive Legal Aspects of Teacher's Discipline*, Floyd G. Delon, No. 2 NOLPE, Topeka, Kansas, 1972, p. 6.

Figure 2

FLOW DIAGRAM FOR CERTIFICATION

DIVISION OF TEACHER EDUCATION AND CERTIFICATION

Incoming Applications and Information

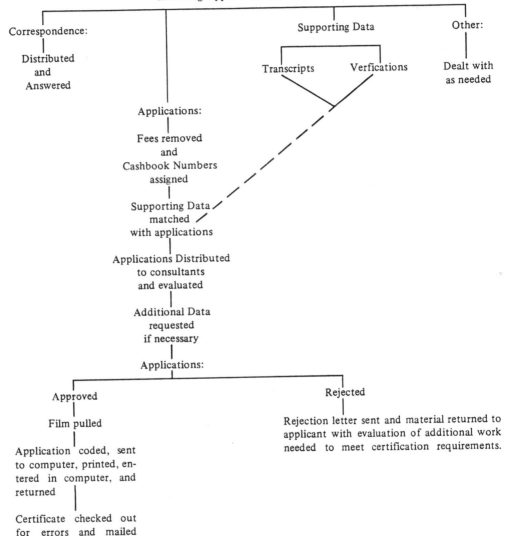

grounds are discussed in Chapter 2). Those most frequently listed are immorality, incompetency, neglect of duty, insubordination, and refusal to obey school board regulations.

A criminal conviction may result in the denial or revocation of a teaching certificate. A number of states expressly require that the certificate be revoked for "conviction of a felony or crime involving moral turpitude." For example, in California, a male teacher who was found guilty of homosexual activity on a public beach contended that the state board of education failed to establish any rational connection between that conduct and his fitness to teach. Among other things, he claimed that revocation of his license would be double punishment since he had been punished by the state. The court ruled in favor of the board and his license to teach was revoked.[17]

Moral turpitude is not limited to sexual connotations. For example, a California court upheld the dismissal of a teacher based on a *nolo contendere* plea to a charge of possession of marijuana, coupled with extensive testimony as to the potential adverse effect upon other teachers and students if the teacher were allowed to continue in the profession.

Summary

Article 1, Section 10 of the Constitution of the United States reads in part: "No state shall . . . pass any Bill of Attainer, *ex post facto* law, or law impairing the Obligation of Contracts . . ."

Teachers, and usually other professional employees, are employed under term contracts or tenure laws. In practically every state, there is some legislation regarding the employment of teachers. Only in the absence of such legislation is the common law, per se, applicable. In many nontenure areas, legislation provides the length of contract by which teachers may be employed, the procedure to be followed, sometimes the provisions of the contract document, and often the causes to be considered justifiable reasons for dismissal before the end of the contract period. Under such provisions, the statute takes precedence over the contract document.

When dismissed before the end of a term contract, principles of contract law apply, unless superseded by statutory provisions. If dismissal violates the provisions of the statute (or the contract), the dismissal is a breach of contract on the part of the employer and the teacher is entitled to sue for damages; if the provisions of the statute (or the contract) provide for dismissal under specified

---

[17]Sarac v. Board of Education (State), 249 Cal. App. 2d 58, 57 Cal. Rptr. 69 (1967).

circumstances, and the dismissal is consistent with these provisions, there has been no breach of contract.

Any contract for a specified length of time is a term contract. Common law or due process of law redress for breach of contract does not protect a teacher from unwarranted "dismissal" at the end of a contract period; that is not a dismissal in the legal sense, being only failure to renew a term contract. Only by a tenure law is continuity of employment provided.

There are, however, restrictions on types of contracts that may be consummated and guaranteed against impairment. Contracts that are in violation of constitutional provisions, statutes, or public policy are prohibited. Thus, contracts may not be entered into legally that will make state laws inoperative, nor do the obligations of contracts prohibit the state from enacting statutes outlawing undesirable practices. However, contracts entered into by school districts, including teaching contracts, are fully protected under Article 1, Section 10 of the United States Constitution.

Compendium of Cases

I. Where charges of inefficiency against a teacher had been established, the dismissal of the teacher was ordered.[18] The fact that a school psychologist had been rated only once during the nearly three years of employment and that the one rating occurred shortly before her dismissal did not warrant the affirmance of an order of the Secretary of Education reinstating the psychologist as "punishment" of the school district for its failure to make regular ratings of performance where the circumstances did not reveal such a pattern of neglect as had been held to warrant the "punishing of a school district."[19]

II. The witholding of two days' pay from teachers who were not present for the days immediately preceding the opening of school to perform the duties required of them was held to be proper action by a board of education.[20] The withholding of a

---

[18]*In re* Tenure Hearing of Michael F. Secula, Dec. of N.J. Comm'r of Educ. (1977).

[19]Board of School Dir. of the Centennial School Dist. v. Secretary of Educ. 376 A.2d 302 (Pa. Cmwlth. 1977).

[20]Fitzgibbon v. Board of Education of the Twp. of Jefferson, Dec. of N.J. Comm'r of Educ. (1977).

salary increment from a teacher because of excessive absenteeism was held to be proper.[21]

III.   Where a teacher had become involved with a student in connection with the sale of coins, the teacher being the Advisor to the Coin Club; and where, as a result of what the board of education determined to be poor judgment on the part of the teacher in connection with the transaction, the board notified the teacher that his contract would not be renewed; and where the teacher pleaded with the board to reconsider its action and the board then stated it would renew the contract of the teacher on condition that he accept a penalty of the withholding of an increment with the teacher remaining one step behind his regular position on the Salary Guide until he finally reached the maximum step; the action of the board was held not to have been too severe a penalty. In view, however, of the outstanding record of the teacher, it was suggested that the board review its actions to determine whether it might wish to revise the penalty.[22]

IV.   A claim by a teacher that she was entitled to have her contract renewed because she had received excellent evaluations was rejected. It was held that her constitutional rights had not been violated. It was further held that the concern of the board about the severity of grades given by the teacher was legitimate.[23]

V.   Where teachers have served the time period set by law in order to achieve tenure, tenure attaches. A board may not defeat a claim of tenure by giving the teacher the title of "long term substitute" when the teacher is in fact performing the duties of a full-fledged teacher. Once tenure has been achieved, that teacher is entitled to the salary and benefits due a tenured teacher and where a board failed to make such a payment, it will be ordered to compensate the teacher for the benefits denied.[24]

VI.   Six nontenured teachers were laid off due to economic reasons after procedures set forth in the negotiated contract were

---

[21]Williams v. Board of Educ. of the Twp. of Teaneck, Dec. of N.J. Comm'r of Educ. (1977).

[22]DeOld v. Board of Education of the Borough of Verona, Dec. of N.J. Comm'r of Educ. (1977).

[23]Fox v. Board of Education of the Watchung Hills Regional High School District, Dec. of N.J. Comm'r of Educ. (1977).

[24]Levitt v. Board of Education of the City of Newark, Dec. of N.J. Comm'r of Educ., (1977).

complied with. They went to court contending they were entitled to the 60 days' notice provided in the teacher tenure act. The Court held for the board, stating that to make this necessary would be to grant nontenured teachers greater rights than were available to tenured teachers.[25]

VII. Nontenured teacher alleging violation of constitutional rights upon her dismissal had her claim rejected by the court. Teacher felt that the Fourteenth Amendment property right to a job was breached and cited both Board of Regents v. Roth[26] and Perry v. Sinderman.[27] This four year instructor was not denied a property interest since she only had an expectation of employment and she was not stigmatized or deprived of the "liberty" protected by the Fourteenth Amendment since she could get employment elsewhere.[28]

VIII. School boards "hire" and "fire" teachers, not school superintendents. The school superintendent can only recomment. In this case, a part-time teacher was recommended by superintendent for full year employment. However, the school board rejected the appointment. The teacher contended that superintendent's recommendation for employment "automatically re-employed" her.[29]

IX. State Board of Education permanently revoked a teacher's certificate who was arrested on many charges—the most important being "delivery of 114 pounds of marijuana." On appeal, the Florida Court of Appeals insisted that (1) while the statute authorizing dismissal was constitutional (2) the "record was insufficient to sustain action of permanent revocation." Thus, the State Board's action was quashed and remanded for further consideration.[30]

X. Dismissal of teacher for failure to meet prescribed eligibility requirements for certification upheld, because teacher was not deprived of due process. The court cannot intervene in the absence of a constitutional defect although the equities clearly

---

[25]Boyce v. Board of Education of City of Royal Oak, 257 N.W.2d 153 (Mich. 1977).
[26]408 U.S. 562.
[27]408 U.S. 593.
[28]Meyr v. Board of Education Affton School District, 435 F. Supp. 1155 (D. Mo. 1977).
[29]Marsh v. Birmingham Board of Education, 349 So.2d 34 (Ala. 1977).
[30]Fischler v. Askew, 349 So.2d 227 (Fla. App. 1977).

favor the teacher.[31]

XI.   A teacher who made an unauthorized physical examination of a pupil in the absence of the school nurse was found guilty of unprofessional conduct and his dismissal was ordered.[32]

XII.   A teacher who had certification in elementary education at the time of her hiring and who was thereafter assigned to teach vocal music on a part-time basis was held to be entitled to a full time teaching position as an elementary school teacher by reason of her seniority rights.[33]

XIII.   A teacher who falsly took sick leave to accompany a female pupil under eighteen years of age to a State College; who failed to grade papers contrary to the express directions of his Department Head; who improperly graded students contrary to rules and regulations of the school; who took students from the school to a bank without proper authorization; who transported a female student to school in contravention of rules and regulations and of express instructions from superiors; who improperly took a female student off of school property; who improperly issued a pass to a student who was not a member of his class; who failed to report for assigned lunch duty and who failed to give a proper explanation for such failure; who gave false information in connection with an inventory; who permitted his classroom to become littered and permitted damage to occur; who granted awards to students who were not members of his class; who permitted a student to lie across three or four desks contrary to rules and regulations; who permitted property belonging to the board of education to be damaged and destroyed was found to be guilty of unbecoming conduct and his dismissal was ordered.[34]

XIV.   Where a teacher who was participating in a basketball game was pushed from behind by a pupil who was playing in the game, and the teacher turned around and with a single blow of an open hand struck the student on his right cheek causing the student to lose one tooth and suffering serious damage to a second tooth, also causing the student to sustain a bloody nose and a

---

[31]Irizarry v. Anker, 558 F.2d 1122 (2d Cir. 1977).

[32]*In re* William Simpson, Dec. of N.J. Comm'r of Educ. (1978).

[33]Large v. Board of Education of the Borough of Roseland, Dec. of N.J. Comm'r of Educ. (1978).

[34]*In re* Chris A. Gervasio, Dec. of N.J. Comm'r of Educ. (1978).

black eye; the conduct of the teacher was held to be cause for discharge.[35]

XV.   One may not automatically gain continuing contract status (tenure) by the act of voluntarily accepting a term contract that does not expire until the statutory probation period has been passed.[36]

XVI.   Where during a school board hearing regarding termination of a tenure teacher, a settlement was reached including stipulations that were fulfilled, the teacher could not subsequently attack the arrangement as being against policy because he had waived some statutory rights.[37]

XVII.   Associate Superintendent of Personnel has no authority to accept a tenured teacher's resignation, only the school board may do so. In this case, a continuing contract teacher, "after an altercation" with an administrator, and upon advice by the Associate Superintendent of Personnel and a school board member to either resign or be fired, mailed a letter of resignation to the Associate Superintendent. Three days later he hand delivered a letter to the Associate Superintendent withdrawing the resignation. Two days later the Associate Superintendent notified the teacher by letter accepting his resignation. The "acceptance was without authority of law."[38]

XVIII.   Teacher was successful in bid to regain job he was fired from based upon board of education's failure to provide a hearing as to why his contract was terminated. In addition the jury awarded the teacher $17,000 for mental anguish because of the termination and back wages of $16,440. Exemplary damages of $25,000 were awarded teacher against superintendent and principal for an inaccurate, nonfactual, not objective, and grossly unfair evaluation. Teacher's attorney was likewise awarded his fees based upon board's unreasonable and obdurate obstinacy in failure to accord a proper hearing.[39]

---

[35]McLaughlin v. Machias School Committee, 385 A.2d 53 (Sup. Ct. of Me. 1978).

[36]Shankle v. Board of Education of Ontario Local School, 374 N.E.2d 648 (Ohio App. 1977).

[37]Abramovich v. Board of Education of Cent. School District. 403 N.Y.S.2d 919 (App. Div. 1978).

[38]Alexander v. Alabama State Tenure Comm., 358 So.2d 1032 (Ala. App. 1978).

[39]Burnaman v. Bay City Independent School District, 445 F. Supp. 927 (S.D. Tex. 1978).

Chapter 4

TORT LIABILITY

The truism that every person should be responsible for his wrongful conduct is fundamental in our society. However, there is one exception: those persons under some legal disability, such as children below the age of reason, are not legally held responsible for their wrongful conduct. An offense against the state is a crime and constitutes a positive or negative breach of some duty an individual owes to the community.

A tort is a civil wrong that causes injury to person or property. Tort may be direct physical injury to a person (assault or battery) or to do damage to a person's reputation (libel or slander). The purpose of the law of tort is to adjust losses arising out of human activities and to "afford compensation for injuries sustained by one person as the result of the conduct of another."[1]

In determining whether a given act constitutes a tort, the following elements must be shown to exist to establish a legal cause of action:

1. A duty or obligation requiring one to conform to a certain standard of conduct so as to protect others against unreasonable risk.
2. A failure on one's part to act in a manner that conforms to the standard of conduct required.
3. Injury to another caused by one's failure to act in the manner required.
4. Actual damage or loss to the person or injury of another as a result of the failure to act.

---

[1]Prosser, William L.: *Handbook on the Law of Torts*, 3rd ed. St. Paul, Minn: West Publishing Co., 1964, p. 6.

When a tort is alleged to have been committed, the person who claims to have been injured must establish that:

1. The defendant had a duty to protect the complainant.
2. The defendant failed to perform that duty, i.e. failed to protect the complainant from injury.
3. There was a breach of duty by the defendant that was the proximate cause of the injury.

Unless these three points can be proven, the defendant will not be held liable for injuries sustained by the complainant.

Defenses to Tort

The law recognizes two general types of defenses to tort actions—no legal duty and no breach of legal duty. The test of no legal duty is whether the plaintiff had a cause of action, i.e. whether the essential components of an actionable tort are present. The second type of test includes the defense of (1) contributory negligence, (2) voluntary assumption of risk, and (3) privilege.

In the defense of no legal duty, the party charged with tortious conduct alleges that he was under no legal duty to the party whose person or property was damaged.

In the defense of no breach of legal duty, the party charged concedes the existence of a legal duty but alleges that his conduct did not constitute a breach of that duty. There is no breach of legal duty if the party charged shows by competent evidence that he exercised that degree of care required by law.

In the defense of contributory negligence, the party charged concedes that he may not have exercised the proper care, but alleges that the party whose person or property was damaged also failed to exercise the proper care for his own safety or the safety of his property.

In the defense of voluntary assumption of risk, the party charged alleges that the law recognizes in him a privilege to engage in the conduct that has caused the complained of damage. There are two types of privileges: absolute and qualified.

Statute of Limitation

For a liability suit to lie against a defendant, the action must be filed within a certain specified period of time. Statutes of limitations fix the limit of time within which various suits may be filed. These laws vary from state to state. Statutes of limitation are intended to protect defendants from false claims and to avoid the difficulty in obtaining evidence that is present with a significant time lapse. It is generally agreed that the statute of limitations does not begin to run until there has been some damage to the plaintiff; it is less clear when the cause of action, and thus the statute of limitations, does begin.[2]

In some instances, the courts have held that the statute did not begin to run until the damage is manifest, and in other instances, the courts have permitted an extension of the statute.[3]

Liability of School Districts for Negligence

The common law principles, almost universally applied by American courts, are that school districts and municipalities are not liable to pupils for injuries resulting from the negligence of the officers, agents, or employees of the district or the municipality,[4] nor does it matter that the injury was sustained while the pupil was off the school premises,[5] or while being transported to or from school.[6] In order to hold a school board liable in such cases, there must be a statute expressly making it liable, and a statute providing that a school district may sue and be sued does not overcome the common law immunity.

Today, this immunity is being challenged as never before, and a few states have abrogated it, some by statute and some by judicial decree.[7]

The following cases will cite the immunity of school districts. In Ohio, a principal required a pupil, without the consent of his parents, to submit to an examination and treatment by a dentist

---

[2]Prosser, W. and J. Wade: *Cases and Materials on Tort*, 5th ed. 1971, p. 551.

[3]Stein v. Highland Park Independent School District, 540 S.W.2d 551 (Tex. Civ. App. 1976).

[4]Meyer v. Board of Education, 9 N.J. 46, 88 Atl.2d 761.

[5]Whitfield v. East Baton Rouge Parish School Board, 43 So.2d (La.) 47.

[6]Wright v. Consolidated School District, 162 Okla. 110, 19 Pac.2d 369.

[7]Garber, Lee O.: "Origin of Governmental Immunity from Tort Doctrine." In Lee O. Garber (Ed.): *Yearbook of School Law*. Danville, Ill: The Interstate Printers and Publishers, 1964, p. 235.

employed by the board of education. In extracting a tooth, the dentist fractured the pupil's jawbone, but the courts refused to allow damages against the school district, notwithstanding the charge that the dentist was negligent and incompetent.[8] Similarly, it was held that the school district was not liable in the following cases: (1) where a pupil was injured on school grounds by a motor truck negligently driven by an employee of the board of education;[9] (2) where a pupil was injured by falling into a pail containing hot water, caustic acid, and chemical compounds, which had been placed in a passage way to be used in scrubbing the floor;[10] (3) where a pupil was injured while operating a buzz saw, the injury growing out of the failure of the teacher to require the pupil to use the safeguards provided by the board of education.[11]

Many reasons have been assigned in support of the common law rule of nonliability of school districts for the negligent acts of their officers and employees. Bolmeier[12] cites ten:

SOVEREIGNTY. The school district exercises sovereign power as it acts through the board of education and is as immune from suit as the sovereign itself.

STARE DECISIS. The principle of tort nonliability for school districts has been determined by the settled rule of common law that quasicorporations are not liable for the torts of their officers, agents, and employees committed during acts performed solely for the benefit of the public except when such liability is provided by statute.

GOVERNMENTAL FUNCTION. The school district is not liable for torts of its officers, agents, or employees analogous to the liability enforced against municipal corporations for proprietary activities because it exercises governmental functions for the benefit of the public and has no proprietary function for its own corporate benefit.

---

[8]Edward, Newton: "The Courts and the Public Schools." Chicago: The University of Chicago Press, p. 399; Board of Education v. McHenry, 106 Ohio St. 357, 140 N.E. 169.

[9]Dick v. Board of Education, 238 S.W. (Mo.) 1073.

[10]Juul v. School District of Manitowoc, 168 Wis. 111, 169 N.W. 309.

[11]Johnson v. Board of Education, 206 N.Y.S. 610.

[12]Bolmeier, Edward C.: *The School in the Legal Structure.* Cincinnati: The W. H. Anderson Company, 1973, pp. 138-139.

LEGAL INABILITY TO PAY. The school district cannot be liable for tort because it has no corporation fund for which it can legally satisfy tort judgments and no method whereby it can legally raise funds for this purpose.

INVOLUNTARY AGENCY. The school district is not liable in a tort action because it is an involuntary statutory agency, of limited powers and prescribed duties, and without choice of whether it will function.

RESPONDEAT SUPERIOR. The school district is not liable for the torts of its officers, agents, or employees because the principle of *respondeat superior* (owner, employee, or agent is liable for acts of his servants or employees) does not apply to school districts.

ULTRA VIRES. The school district cannot be made subject to tort liability, because any tortious act of its officers, agents, or employees is *ultra vires* the powers of the district.

IMMUNITY AS CHARITY. School districts should enjoy the torts immunity traditionally accorded to charitable institutions.

IMPAIRMENT OF SCHOOL FUNCTIONS. School district's tort liability is undesirable on the grounds of public policy because it would result in multiplicity of suits and serious impairment of the functions of some schools.

PROHIBITIVE COST. Tort liability of school districts is undesirable because it would increase the financial burden of maintaining the schools.[13]

The court recognizes defenses other than immunity and in some instances removes cases from the jury's hands to issue summary judgments for the defendants.[14]

Negligence

Negligence is the most common tort. Negligence, in the absence of statute, is defined as "failure to act as a reasonable prudent person would act under the particular circumstances."[15]

---

[13]Also see Fuller, E.E.: "Reasons Given by Courts for School District Immunity." *American School Board Journal, 103:*23-25, Nov. 1941.

[14]Shannon v. Addison Trail High School District No. 88, 33 Ill. App.3d 953, 339 N.E.2d 372 (1975).

[15]Good, Carter V.: *Dictionary of Education,* 3rd ed. New York: McGraw-Hill Book Co., 1973, p. 383.

There are four degrees of negligence:

1. Negligence, actionable—the non-performance of a legal duty by the failure to act as a prudent person or the failure to exercise an ordinary amount of care, thus resulting in a damage to another.
2. Negligence, comparative—that doctrine in the law that compares the degree of negligence of the parties involved.
3. Negligence, contributory—failure by an injured person to use ordinary care, which is a concurrent cause with the negligence of the injury in producing the injury.
4. Negligence, simple—negligence that is neither gross nor wanton but merely a failure to exercise ordinary care.[16]

Negligence is the tort most frequently alleged to have been committed by school personnel. In order to prove negligence, the injured party must show that the defendant owed a duty (due care) to protect the complainant from injury, that the defendant failed to exercise that duty, that this failure was the direct (proximate) cause of the injury, and that actual loss or damage resulted.[17]

Redress for Injury through Negligence of Teacher or School Board

The extent to which a teacher is liable for injuries sustained by a pupil depends upon the common law principles of negligence. Public school teachers have no special immunity because they are public employees. In fact, they may be held even more accountable than the ordinary person, because pupils are in their care and they have the duty to prevent pupil injuries so far as possible.

Some injuries are caused by what the law calls a "pure accident"; that is, it was unforeseeable, unavoidable, and no one was to blame. Other injuries are caused by another person's negligence in allowing or in not preventing the injury. If a teacher's negligence can be proven, he can be held for damages in a tort action brought by the pupil or his parents. If the teacher can prove that there was no negligence but the injury was caused by a

---

[16]*Supra* note 15.

[17]See Delon, Floyd G.: *Legal Controls on Teacher Conduct: Teacher Education.* Topeka, Kansas: NOLPE, 1977. Also *supra* note 2, pp. 150-151.

pure accident, there is no recovery of damages. It is, therefore, necessary to examine what might be called negligence by the courts.

Negligence at law is any conduct that falls below standards for the protection of others against unreasonable risk of harm. Negligence may be acts of commission or omission, and liability is conditioned upon both the character of the conduct and the nature of the results. The amount of caution required is proportionate to the amount of threatened or apparent danger.

The first test to determine if there has been negligence is the test of foreseeability. When a reasonable, prudent person could have foreseen the harmful consequences of his act, the actor, in disregarding the foreseeable consequences, is liable for negligent conduct. This is the general rule. Appying it to the teacher-pupil relationship, we may say that if a reasonably prudent teacher could have foreseen that a pupil might be injured by some act of his own or another person, the teacher is liable if he disregards these foreseeable consequences.

There may be many antecedent events leading to an injury, each in its major or minor way contributing to the cause, but some of these antecedent events have no legal bearing on the cause of the injury. The one or more causes without which the injury would not have happened is or are the actual causes among all the antecedent events. Among these actual causes, the legal cause is that cause which in the natural and continuous sequence of events produced the result, provided that there has been no interference of an independent superceding cause.

A negligent person is relieved of legal responsibility if some other event breaks the connection between his act and the harm done, in such a way as to be considered by the court as a superseding cause of the harm, but the determination that an act is a superseding cause involves complicated legal principles.

When a teacher is sued for negligent conduct that has caused injury to a pupil, one defense may be contributory negligence. Contributory negligence is conduct on the part of the injured person that falls below the standard to which he should conform for his own protection, and which is a contributing factor bringing about the person's injury.

Although a teacher is not liable for pupil injuries unless it can be shown that the teacher was negligent, once negligence has been proved, there are far-reaching implications of liability. For example, a person whose negligence has caused an injury to another may be held liable also for physical harm resulting from fright or shock or other similar and immediate emotional disturbances caused by the injury; for additional bodily harm resulting from acts done by third persons in rendering aid irrespective of whether the subsequent acts are done in a proper or negligent manner; for a disease contracted because of lowered vitality resulting from the injury; or for harm sustained in a subsequent accident that would not have happened had the injured's bodily efficiency not been impaired by the negligent person. Furthermore, a teacher may be liable for injuries resulting from his conduct where prior physical condition of the pupil is unknown.

The burden of proving negligence rests with the plaintiff, while the existence of negligence and the amount of compensable damage arising therefrom are questions to be decided by the courts.

The following illustrates the wide range of suits that have been filed claiming negligence. Teachers have been involved in lawsuits when:[18]

1. The teacher's lesson plans left for a substitute failed to warn of the mischievous nature of a particular student;
2. A physical education teacher failed to warn high school students enrolled in his gym class that there were dangers in the sport of boxing;
3. An elementary school teacher failed to inspect and warn students of potentially dangerous or faulty playground equipment;
4. A school district did not publish rules of bicycle safety;
5. A teacher made a derogatory statement about the conduct of a pupil's parent;
6. Students in an auto repair shop did not check the gas tank before welding on a car;
7. A student died as a result of injuries of unknown causes

---

[18]Strickland, Rennard, Janet Freaier Phillips, and William R. Phillips: *Avoiding Teacher Malpractice.* New York: Hawthorn Books, Inc., 1976, pp. 12-13.

suffered behind the school building at an after-school dance;

8. The guard on a saw in the machine shop was defective;
9. A student attacked a fellow student in the hall during passing period;
10. A delinquent student stabbed a classmate in a classroom before school;
11. A teacher assigned a task that a student was too immature or inexperienced to carry out successfully;
12. A teacher sent a pupil on errands and used the pupil as a student helper to open windows;
13. A teacher was employed during vacation in a bar owned by her own husband.

Defamation of Character

Defamation encompasses the twin torts of libel and slander and involves statements made to a third party that damages another's reputation or good name.

Any words tending to harm a person's reputation so as to lower the person in the estimation of the community or to deter people from associating with him or her are "defamatory words." Under certain circumstances, such words form the basis for a suit in which the person so injured seeks damages and the clearing of his reputation. Defamation may be a statement of fact, as "Mr. X did thus and so"; it may be the opinion based upon facts known, assumed, or undisclosed, as "I think Mr. X should be fired for the betterment of the school."

False charges of this type tend to defame the teacher's character and make it more difficult to secure other employment. Therefore, the question arises as to when a teacher can obtain legal redress from the responsible persons in a suit for defamation of character. In general, it must be remembered that only under certain circumstances will the court redress such a wrong.

Communication, oral or written, is called publication. A court will not consider a slander case unless the words are of a certain nature. Written defamation, libel, is more easily redressed in the law courts than spoken defamation. Libel is frequently actionable even though the same words if spoken would not be actionable without special damage; that is, when the words are written, no injury to reputation need be proved. The mere publication of libel may be sufficient to maintain the action.

Slander

The words that historically were considered slanderous were (1) those imputing the commission of certain crimes; (2) any imputation affecting a person's reputation for skill in his business, office, trade, profession, or occupation that tended to cause his position to be prejudicially affected. To these three classes of slander another class has been added in modern times: words imputing unchastity to a woman. In these classes of defamation, no special injury need be proved: the words are enough. If the defamation does not fall into one of these classes, special injury must be proved: the words are not enough.

An action for slander will lie if one is accused of committing a crime that is punishable by imprisonment. The words to be actionable in this class must charge that the person has committed the crime; that he is a potential criminal is not a slanderous charge unless special damage can be proved. If the school law provides for discipline of a teacher convicted of a crime, conviction is conclusive of guilt for this purpose, and the teacher, even though injured in reputation thereby, cannot sue for an accusation based upon a fact.

If a male teacher unjustly accused of unchastity can show special damage, or that the defamation injured his reputation as a teacher, or that the conduct of which he is accused constitutes a statutory crime of which he is innocent, he can sue for slander. A woman, however, need not show special damage or any other evidence than the untruth of the statements.

An imputation of unchastity may be inferred from any words that would naturally be understood by the hearers even though the charge is not made in explicit terms. However, imputations of immodesty that do not imply unchastity are not actionable, and innuendos cannot be interpreted beyond their reasonable meaning.

False words spoken by a teacher about one of his pupils would be actionable unless the slanderous words were communicated under privileged circumstances. A teacher's report to the principal or other school official would certainly be privileged, as would also a communication to the pupil's parents or guardian.

There would be no privilege, however, if a teacher slandered a pupil in the presence of other pupils, before the general public, to parents not involved in the situation, or to teachers not teaching the pupil. The same distinctions would prevail between words actionable per se and those on account of which special injury must be proved in order to obtain damages.

Teachers are frequently asked for letters of recommendation on former students. Such letters are considered confidential, and honest comments are sometimes encouraged by prospective employers that they may better judge the potential worth of an applicant for employment. Dare a teacher write a derogatory letter without subjecting himself to a suit for slander? If the letter expresses the teacher's honest opinion, reasonably based upon evidence that convinced the teacher of the truth of his estimate of the pupil and is not written with malicious intent to injure him, the communication under these circumstances is privileged; provided, of course, that the teacher does not show the letter to any other person, mails it to the prospective employer, and has no reason to know that any but the prospective employer will read it upon receipt. Communication by the employer after receipt of the letter may constitute slander on the employer's part, depending upon the circumstances, but does not reflect back to the teacher who wrote the letter, unless the teacher could have anticipated such publication. The same principles apply to letters of recommendation written by principals and superintendents concerning teachers.

Guidelines Regarding Libel and Slander

1. Limit discussion of and written statements about individual students and fellow educators to statements that you know or reasonably know to be true.
2. Limit discussion of and written statements about individual students and fellow educators to statements that have a valid educational purpose.
3. If you must make possibly damaging and controversial statements you know to be true and you believe to have an educationally valid purpose, retain the evidence from which you drew your conclusions.

4. Ask yourself if the evidence of truth of a damaging statement would hold up in court. Ask yourself if it is the sort of evidence that a jury of your neighbors would believe. If not, reconsider making your statements.

5. Remember that parents and pupils have expanded rights to examine documents under the Buckley Amendment. Consider that third persons outside the school may see or hear your statements.

6. Never make statements or write reports in the heat of anger. Delay saying potentially dangerous, damaging, or libelous things.

7. Whenever possible talk directly to persons involved to determine the source of damaging statements and to verify the truth.

8. Before making or writing any statement, ask if it holds another up to contempt, hatred, or ridicule. If so, be especially sure of the truth of the statement and of the educational purpose in repeating it.

9. Never, never expect that statements made in confidence to pupils, or in the teachers' lounge, will not be repeated.[19]

Control of Pupils' Conduct

Pupils have the responsibility of obeying the school laws and the rules and regulations of the state and local governing officials; they have the duty of submitting to the orders of their teachers and other school authorities. Failure to do so may result in corporal punishment, suspension, or expulsion. Corporal punishment usually falls within the scope of the teacher's authority; suspension and expulsion are usually within the discretionary powers of the school board. In the power to regulate pupil's conduct, the teacher stands somewhat *in loco parentis*; that is, the teacher is conditionally privileged to take disciplinary steps under certain circumstances and for certain purposes.

Corpus Juris Secundum (79 C. J. S. 493) gives the following explanation of the position of the teacher with regard to disciplinary control of pupils:

---

[19]*Supra* note 18, p. 85.

> As a general rule a school teacher, to a limited extent at least, stands *in loco parentis* to pupils under his charge, and may exercise such powers of control, restraint, and correction over them as may be reasonably necessary to enable him properly to perform his duties as teacher and accomplish the purposes of education, and subject to such limitations and prohibitions as may be defined by legislative enactment. . . .

State statutes that deal with corporal punishment of pupils are of several definite types. In the District of Columbia and New Jersey, corporal punishment is prohibited by law. Many local school districts have so ruled also, by school board regulation. In the absence of prohibitory legislation, state or local, a teacher may administer corporal punishment because he stands *in loco parentis*. There are certain common law principles in this regard, e.g. that the punishment be not unreasonable, not excessive in view of the age and sex of the pupil, not excessive in view of the gravity of the offense, not administered maliciously. These common law principles are either written into statutes or implied in more general statutory language.

Almost all states have laws forbidding cruelty to children, and if corporal punishment administered by a school teacher be excessive or administered with a dangerous instrument or in an improper manner, the teacher is liable to apprehension under such laws, which usually provide a penalty or a fine or imprisonment.

A third type of law bearing on the teacher's authority consists of sanctions for moderate and reasonable punishment through the definition of assault and battery or homicide in the penal codes of a number of states. These laws define assault and battery as the use of force or violence upon or toward another person, with the proviso that force or violence shall not be considered assault and battery when commited in certain instances, including the lawful exercise of authority to restrain a pupil. Even death of a pupil from corporal punishment may be excused in law if the teacher's conduct was within the limits set forth in certain statutes defining homicide.

When Is Corporal Punishment Reasonable and Proper?

The following characteristics of reasonable and proper punishment are offered as guides:

1. It is conformance with statutory enactments.
2. It is for the purpose of correction and without malice.
3. The pupil knows wherein he has erred and is thus aware of the reason for the punishment.
4. It is not cruel nor excessive and leaves no permanent mark or injury.
5. It is suited to the age and sex of the pupil.
6. It is administered in the pupil-teacher relationship.

Miscellaneous Tort Cases

Under the familiar principles of tort law, the concrete duty imposed by this attitude is that teachers and administrators must act toward pupils as would a reasonable, prudent person or parent under the circumstances. If school personnel have acted as a reasonable, prudent parent under the circumstances and nevertheless a child is injured, the teacher or administrator cannot be held responsible.

A case in point, a pupil in 1940 at the Altona Central School, in Clinton County, recovered a judgment against a physical education teacher in that school, on account of injuries he received while participating in a required physical activity, boxing with another pupil. These young men were instructed by defendant to box three rounds of one minute each with a minute of rest intervening. Following a blow on the temple, plaintiff became dizzy and staggered, had a headache for a considerable length of time, and finally became unconscious.

The plaintiff subsequently underwent two operations. However, the operations did not restore him to full physical capacity. In awarding the settlement, the courts held, "it is the duty of a teacher to exercise reasonable care to prevent injuries. Pupils should be warned before being permitted to engage in a dangerous and hazardous exercise." The testimony, of both boxers, indicated that the teacher failed in his duties in this regard and that he was negligent, and the plaintiff was entitled to recover for damages.

Teacher Liability for Inadequate Supervision

Parents have entrusted their children to public schools for instructional purposes as the compulsory attendance laws direct.

The law anticipates that the children will be protected and their best interests looked after by those in charge.

The standard of supervisory conduct on the part of the teacher is that prudence and care which the normal parent might exercise under the same or similar conditions. A teacher may not assume, however, that the mere fact that it was an accident will absolve him of a charge of negligence. Where a known hazard exists, the teacher has the duty of foreseeing the danger, and preventing an accident before it occurs.

Sometimes a pupil suffers an injury while the teacher is absent from the classroom. Courts seek a causal relationship between the teacher's absence and the injury; for a charge of negligence to lie, the teacher's absence must be the proximate cause of the injury.

The teacher is not expected to exercise extraordinary or unremitting supervision; he cannot continuously keep under his eye all the students in his care, and sometimes accidents occur when the teacher is "looking the other way." In such cases, if the general supervision is held to be adequate, no negligence attaches.

Teachers will do well to minimize the number of times they must be absent from their posts, inasmuch as such absences may amount legally to failure to provide adequate supervision.

Liability Waivers

When planning certain school activities such as athletic events, field trips, etc., the school administration may require written parental consent before permitting a student to participate. As far as relieving the teacher or school of tort liability, such parental permission slips have little value. The only value of the permission slip, in addition to its public relations worth, lies in the knowledge that the parent knows of the activity and has indicated a willingness for his child to participate in it. The slip in no way absolves the teacher of his responsibility to exercise the usual care in protecting the welfare of the child.

School Safety Patrols

It is well settled that school districts should not assign pupils to duties that are adult tasks or that place pupils in unnecessary, hazardous positions, neither should the school assign pupils to patrol territory outside the limits of the school's property.

Field Trips

School supervised field trips have become an important part of the school curriculum. No case has been found in which it was sought to hold the teacher or principal liable for pupil injury while on a field trip. All reported cases were instituted by the injured child or his parents against the agency visited wherein the injury occurred. Generally, courts have ruled that the recovery depends upon whether the pupils are on the premises solely for their own benefit, or whether the host organization also derives some substantial benefit from the visit.

Administrators and teachers should plan carefully for field trips in the full realization that pupil injury may result. Students should be adequately chaperoned while away from school.

Errands

It is well settled that a teacher may be held liable for injuries to a pupil on errands, or to third parties on whom the pupil inflicts injury. Pupils should be sent on errands away from school only in an emergency, and then only when an adult is not available.

Transportation in Privately Owned Cars

The courts have consistently ruled that the teacher may be held liable for damages while transporting school pupils, even though the trip is a regular part of the teacher's duties. Teachers should use extreme caution in using their own or others' cars for transportation of school pupils; when in doubt, consult an attorney.

Medical Treatment of Pupils

In general, the power of the school district is limited to examination and diagnosis only; a board may not provide treatment for pupils in the public schools as a part of the regular school program.

When a child becomes ill or injured at school, it is the duty of the teacher to call the school nurse or the child's parents for medical treatment by the family physician. Failure to provide promptly for the child's safety may result in a charge of negligence against the teacher. However, under no circumstances should the teacher attempt medical treatment of any more than a first aid nature, and then, only in case of an emergency.

Avoidance of Tort Liability

Inasmuch as the question of tort liability of the school district and its employees rests almost exclusively on the element of foreseeability, the importance of careful staff planning to make the school a safe place for pupils cannot be overemphasized.

Five states have adopted statutes requiring or permitting boards of education to come to the aid of school personnel who are found liable for damages in pupil injury cases. Increasingly, school boards are obtaining liability insurance at public expense to cover instances where suit is brought because of the negligence of school personnel for pupil injury.

Additionally, a number of teacher's associations are making available, as part of their membership, liability insurance for teacher protection against negligence charges.

Summary

Any legal action regarding teacher liability for pupil injury would fall in the category of tortious action. A tort is defined as a civil (not criminal) wrong committed against the person or property of another, independent of contract.

The legal test of a tortious act is (1) the existence of a legal duty of one person to another, (2) a breach of that duty, (3) and a causal link between the breach and the distress of the injured party. Thus, as a matter of law, the courts will ask the following three questions whenever a person alleges that a tort has been committed against him:

1. Did the defendant owe the plaintiff a duty?
2. Was there a breach of the duty owed?
3. Was the breach the proximate cause of the plaintiff's injury?

A school district is not liable for the negligent acts of its agents, servants, and officers, unless its immunity has been modified or abrogated by the legislature. The ancient doctrine of sovereign immunity (the King can do no wrong) has provided the common law basis that still remains in a majority of states, an exception being the State of Illinois.

However, legislative action and court decisions of recent years indicate a trend in the direction of denouncing the theory of sovereign immunity and holding school districts liable for their torts. Courts have tended to favor the injured party.

The immunity from tort liability that school districts may enjoy does not extend to the district's employees. The individual employees may be held liable for torts arising out of their own negligence.

Negligence is defined as the omission to do something that a reasonable person, guided by those considerations that ordinarily regulate human affairs, would do, or the doing of something which a reasonable and prudent person would not do. Negligence is thus viewed as the failure to use such care and caution as a hypothetically reasonable and prudent person would ordinarily have exercised under the same or similar conditions.

Since the teacher is expected to act as a prudent person would act under the circumstances, foreseeability is an important aspect of negligence cases. If there is a known hazard, the teacher is expected to instruct the students thoroughly as to the dangers involved. Generally, the determination of negligence is for the jury, and it seems that, in these cases, negligence is what the jury says it is.

Tort Case Summaries

ACTION BY SCHOOL DISTRICT APPEALING VERDICT FOR STUDENT INJURED DURING TRAMPOLINE COURSE. The school board urged that the student, in order to recover, was bound to prove willful and wanton conduct, rather than negligence only, in supervision of students. The contention was based on a school code provision stating that teachers stand "in the relation of parents" to students in disciplinary matters. The board also urged that the verdict against it should have been set aside when the jury, at the same time, found in favor of the trampoline instructor. *Held:* For the student. The school code did not require application of the *in loco parentis* standard except in disciplinary matters; thus proof of negligence was sufficient. The verdict against the board did not depend on a verdict against the trampoline instructor, since acts of negligence on the part of the board—independent of acts of the teacher—were alleged and proven.[20]

ACTION BY FATHER AND SON AGAINST THE SCHOOL BOARD FOR DAMAGES RESULTING FROM A BEATING BY A TEACHER. A student alleged that a physical education teacher at a junior high school during a class period struck him. Suit was filed against the school board alleging that the willful and wanton conduct of the board through its agent caused the injury. The school board contended that it was not amenable to suit as it was not a legal entity or corporate body of the status that could be sued and that the proper defendant in this case was the school district, which just happened to be immune from suit. *Held:* For the school board. A school board through its members is only a managerial tool. The school district is the corporate body that may be amenable to suit, but in this case it is immune from suit.[21]

ACTION BY THE MOTHER FOR THE WRONGFUL DEATH OF HER CHILD WHO WAS STRUCK BY A TRUCK AFTER WANDERING AWAY FROM A KINDERGARTEN PLAYGROUND. The child during a school lunch period after being released to the playground by school personnel prior to the commencement of class wandered through a hole in a chain-link fence surrounding the area (the hole having existed for several months) onto a busy street and ran into a truck sustaining fatal injuries. Having settled with the truck driver during the trial, the mother continued the action against the District of Columbia, alleging that it had a duty to protect small children against the hazard of a busy thoroughfare 120 feet away, that the school was negligent in providing supervision and liable for the acts of its agents, and that the breach of duty was the proximate cause of the child's demise. *Held:* For the mother. The District of Columbia in the

---

[20]Chilton v. Cook County School Dist. No. 207, Maine Tp., 325 N.E.2d 666 (Ill. Dist Ct. App. 1975); *see also* Wilson v. Kroll, 326 N.E.2d 94 (Ill. Dist. Ct. App. 1975); Maxwell v. Santa Fe Public Schools, 534 P.2d 307 (N. Mex. Ct. App. 1975).

[21]Foster v. Cobb County Board of Education, 213 S.E. 2d 38 (Ga. Ct. App. 1975).

operation of schools and playgrounds is performing ministerial
functions and is without the protection of sovereign immunity.
The school has a duty to protect young children from a busy street
120 feet from a school playgrund. The school has a duty to
provide for the safety of children by ensuring that they are always
adequately supervised. The District is liable for the torts of its
employees when they are acting within the scope of their
employment.[22]

ACTION BY PARENTS FOR INJURIES TO THEIR CHILD SUS-
TAINED ON SCHOOL GROUNDS AFTER SCHOOL HOURS AND
NOT A PART OF SCHOOL-RELATED ACTIVITIES. The child
received a severe shock and injuries from an exposed wire of
which the school had no notice while she was accompanying her
parents and brother who was using the school parking lot to drive
his go-cart. Neither of the children attended the school. The issue
was the duty owed to the child by the school board to provide safe
premises. *Held:* For the school board. The board owed no duty to
the child who was, at best, a licensee. The board's sole duty was to
abstain from intentional or wanton injury. Since the board had
no knowledge of the exposed wires or the child's presence on the
school grounds, it did not violate any duty it owed her.[23]

ACTION BY STUDENT APPEALING AWARD FOR INJURIES
SUSTAINED BY FELLOW STUDENT IN AN AUTO ACCIDENT
WHILE RETURNING FROM A BAND CONCERT. The fellow
student was injured when the car driven by the appellant
overturned. The injured student sued the driver and also sued the
board of education, its band director and its insurer, alleging he
was forced to ride with the driver-student because of failure by
school officials to provide adequate bus transportation. The
injured student reached a settlement agreement with the insurer
of the board. The driver-student urged that the amount of the
settlement should be deducted from the amount of the jury's
award against him and that the injured student was a guest,
rather than a passenger, in his car. *Held:* For the driver-student in
part. The amount of the settlement was deductible from the
award against the driver-student, since the plaintiff can recover

[22]Ballard v. Polly, 387 F. Supp. 895 (D.C. 1975).
[23]Fitzgerald v. Montgomery County Board of Education, 336 A.2d 795 (Md. Ct. of Spec. App. 1975).

only once of the same damages. The evidence was sufficient, however, to establish that the injured student was a passenger and not a guest, since a rider is a passenger when transportation is furnished for mutual business or material interests of both rider and driver. The court noted that the band received money for its performance and that the students could expect to receive material benefits in the form of awards stemming from the concert.[24]

ACTION TO RECOVER FOR THE DEATH OF ONE STUDENT AND INJURY TO ANOTHER DURING FOOTBALL PRACTICE. The plaintiffs sued the school district, superintendent of schools, principal of the high school, and teacher-coaches following the death and injury resulting from heat prostration during football practice. The plaintiffs urged that the football program was a proprietary function and that the district, superintendent, and principal were therefore not immune from suit. They also urged that the teacher-coaches were liable even if the others were immune. *Held:* For the school district in part. Where the football program showed a net operating loss over the last five years, the program was not proprietary and the district, superintendent, and principal were immune from suit. However, the teacher-coaches were not immune from suits based on allegations of personal negligence direct in its effect in individual students.[25]

ACTION BY A STUDENT AGAINST A SCHOOL BOARD FOR INJURIES OCCURRING DURING A VARSITY BASKETBALL PRACTICE. The student while running windsprints during basketball practice crashed through a glass window at the end of the gymnasium and sustained substantial injuries. The school board was alleged to be negligent for not taking sufficient care to prevent such an incident as the window was placed in such a manner so as to create a foreseeable risk of such accidents occurring. The school board raised the defenses of contributory negligence and sovereign immunity even though it had purchased liability insurance. At the close of the plaintiff's evidence, the school board's motion for a directed verdict was granted and appeal was taken. *Held:* For the student, a new trial. The school board waives its sovereign immunity when it purchases liability

---

[24]Whitacre v. Board of Education, 326 N.E.2d 696 (Ohio Ct. App. 1974).
[25]Lovitt v. Concord School District, 228 N.W.2d 479 (Mich. Ct. App. 1975).

insurance. The school board has the burden of proving contributory negligence in the absence of its clear presence.[26]

ACTION BY STUDENT AGAINST SCHOOL DISTRICTS FOR INJURIES SUSTAINED BY THE STUDENT DURING WRESTLING PRACTICE. *Held:* For the school district. The action was barred by the doctrine of governmental immunity. The court found that the doctrine was "legislative-made" and not "court-made" by the legislature's enactment in 1816 of a statute that adopted the common law of England. Thus, abrogation of the doctrine would be left to the legislature. The dissenters urged abrogation, contending that the statute adopting the English common law actually adopted a body of decisional law, rather than substantive statutory rights. They urged that the doctrine was thus subject to abrogation by the courts.[27]

---

[26]Clary v. Alexander County Board of Education, 212 S.E.2d 160 (N.C. 1975).

[27]O'Dell v. School District of Independence, 521 S.W. 2d 403 (Mo. 1975); *see also* Rennie v. Belleview School District, 521 S.W.2d 423 (Mo. 1975).

Chapter 5.

STUDENT RIGHTS AND DUE PROCESS

Introduction

U ntil recently, the local school board and its employees occupied a sanctified position with respect to judicial review; their decisions to suspend or expel students were seldom questioned by the courts. Most challenges to operation had a cold reception by the courts.

For example, in 1890, a Missouri high school student was expelled for "general bad conduct." No specific reason was given for the expulsion and none was required by the courts, which was reluctant to substitute its judgment for that of the school board.[1] In an Illinois case in 1913, a student was expelled for allegedly violating a rule forbidding membership in a fraternity. Although the student denied belonging to a fraternity, his request for a hearing was refused; the court said that under no circumstances— except when fraud, corruption, oppression, or gross injustice is palpably shown—is a court of law authorized to review the decision of a school board of education and to substitute its judgment for the board.[2]

Most courts deferred the question of appropriate punishment to the school board's discretion because education, at one time, was considered a privilege, not a right, and school expulsions were generally not reviewed by the courts. Today education is considered a right that cannot be denied without proper reason

---

[1]Stevenson v. Wheeler City Board of Education, 306 F. Supp. 97 (S.D. Ga., 1969) App. 426 F.2d 1154 (Fifth Cir. 1970).

[2]Smith v. Board of Education, 182 Ill.App. 342 (1913).

and unless proper procedures are followed.[3] Courts now require students be accorded minimum standards of fairness and due process of law in disciplinary procedures that may terminate in suspension[4] or expulsion.[5]

Reasons for Intervention

It is well established that a federal court will not intervene or reverse or enjoin disciplinary actions relevant to a lawful mission of an educational institution unless there appears to be:

1. A deprivation of due process, that is, fundamental concepts of fair play;
2. Invidious indiscrimination, for example, on account of race or religion;
3. Denial of federal rights, constitutional or statutory, protected in the academic community; or
4. Clearly unreasonable, arbitrary or capricious action.[6]

In the field of discipline, scholastic and behavioral norms and expectations, any institution may establish any standards reasonably relevant to the lawful mission, process, or function of an institution to prohibit the exercise of a right guaranteed by the constitution or a law of the United States to a member of the academic community under the circumstances.

However, when a federal court intervenes in educational matters, it must operate under some limitations. One is that the federal courts cannot voluntarily enter a case dealing with the functions of a state educational agency unless a suit is filed individually or is a class action purporting that a right has been violated under the First, Fifth, or Fourteenth Amendments.

A federal court is not required to entertain all suits in which unconstitutional deprivations are asserted. A federal constitutional question must exist not in mere form but in substance, and not in mere assertion but in essence and effect.[7]

---

[3]Goss v. Lopez, 419 U.S. 565, 574 (1975).

[4]Goss v. Lopez, 419 U.S. 565, 579 (1975).

[5]Graham v. Knutzen, 351 F. Supp. 642 (D.C., Neb. 1972); Jordan v. School District of Erie, Ca. No. 34-72 (W.D. Pa, Feb. 1974).

[6]Davis v. Firment, 269 F. Supp. 524 (E.D. La. 1967), aff'd. 408 F.2d 1085 (Fifth Cir. 1969).

[7]Freeman v. Flake, 448 F.2d 258, 261 (Tenth Cir. 1971).

Operational Philosophies

There seems to be two different philosophies used by different courts. One court starts with the premise that the right to appear as one pleases is protected by the constitution, at least to the extent that the local board of education must bear a substantial burden of justification for tampering with a student's rights. The second court seems to begin with the premise that school authorities must be given leeway to establish rules and regulations, and as long as rules and regulations bear reasonable relationship to the atmosphere for learning, it is to be judicially supported.

The Courts and Due Process

The courts on all levels are making and have recently made many decisions concerning student (civil) rights. One of the major issues in question at this time is the issue of due process of law in suspension and expulsion cases. The concept of *in loco parentis* is being shaken. The concept that the school stands *in loco parentis* is at best tenuous and partially misleading. To stand *in loco parentis*, one must assume the *full* duties, responsibilities, and obligations of a parent toward a minor. School teachers and administrators obviously do not support the children in their care, nor do they provide most of the tangible and intangible necessities and securities that the child finds in his/her home.

In fact, school authorities stand *in loco parentis* only to the degree that they may act somewhat like a parent does only some of the time for the purpose of maintaining order in the educational system. Thus, it is misleading to term one narrow function of the school—that is, the disciplinary function—as being a function totally representative of the *in loco parentis* concept.[8]

From the Supreme Court on down, education has been determined to be a fundamental right of all United States citizens.

The California Supreme Court recently held education to be a

---

[8]Manley-Casimir, Michael E.: "Suspension, Expulsion, and Procedural Due Process," *Administrators Notebook*, Vol. 20, p. 4, February, 1972.

fundamental interest. The argument here is that education is so fundamental an interest, that the public school student's freedom to pursue his education should not be restricted or terminated by state action without due process of law. Suspension and expulsion effectively curtail the student's freedom; hence, in these situations schools must develop and apply procedures compatible with due process. As Abe Fortas observes: "Procedure is the bone structure of a democratic society; and the quality of procedural standards which meet general acceptance—the quality of what is tolerable and permissible and acceptable conduct—determines the durability of the society."[9]

The key is that education, being a right, cannot be taken away, other than by due process.

> Since education is a state responsibility, schools fall within the ambit of the due process clause of the Fourteenth Amendment which, in part, prohibits any state from depriving "...any person of life, liberty, or property without due process of law." Boards of Education and their officers are bound by this amendment. In the words of the Supreme Court decision of West Virginia State Board of Education v. Barnette:
>
> > The Fourteenth Amendment, as now applied to the States protects the citizen against the State itself and all of its creatures—boards of education not excepted. These have, of course, important, delicate, and highly discretionary functions, but none that they may not perform within the Bill of Rights. That they are educating the young for citizenship is reason for scrupulous protection of constitutional freedoms of the individual, if we are not to strangle the free mind at its source and teach youth to discount important principles of our government as mere platitudes.[10]

Student Rights in Light of Due Process

Exclusion from school is a penalty with potentially grave consequences for the student. Exclusion may take the form of suspension, which temporarily removes the student from the school, or expulsion, which terminates the student's education at that institution. Either way the decision is serious; even a

---

[9]*Supra*, note 8.
[10]*Supra*, note 8, p. 1-2.

suspension for a few days may lead to failure and to the loss of a whole year; suspension for a longer period or expulsion may result in the student dropping out entirely, with possibly drastic long-term effects.

The stigma of a compulsory withdrawal is likely to follow even the high school student for many years after the incident has been settled in the mind of the institution concerned. Such a procedure almost always involves a permanent notation on the student's record, which may have long-lasting effects on his entrance into college or the job market. If a child is unable to return to school, the economics of a premature withdrawal are just as startling but more tangible evidence of the burden that he must bear.[11]

Removing a student from school is a serious action by the school. (It can, however, be used in a non-punitive context, for example, to reduce tensions or to provide more time than is immediately available to deal with a problem.) Because of its seriousness, only seldom can it be justified when the removal is long-term. One justifiable occasion is when a student's continued presence on the school grounds endangers the school's proper functioning or the safety or well-being of himself or other members of the school community. Another occasion arises when the suspension offers the only effective way of both communicating to the student that his conduct was unacceptable and emphasizing to his parents that they must accept greater responsibility in helping the student meet school standards of acceptable conduct.[12]

Separating a student from school is a poor method of discipline. School expulsion should be avoided, if possible. This does not mean, however, that a disruptive child should be retained in the classroom or that improper conduct should be ignored. When the classroom is not an appropriate place for the child, other provisions should be made for him. When suspension or expulsion is the only means available, due process should be given.

---

[11]*Supra* note 8, p. 1.

[12]Phay, Robert E.: *The Law of Suspension and Expulsion*, Topeka, Kansas: NOLPE, 1975, p. 4.

Due Process

To determine the procedural requirements placed on a school when it completes a suspension or expulsion, one must examine the statutes of that particular state. Due process requirements vary from state to state. For example, Minnesota (1974) adopted a pupil Fair Dismissal Act.[13] This act mandates a pupil must be accorded a conference before he can be suspended or expelled. Three states (Massachusetts, Pennsylvania, and Washington) require a formal hearing. New York requires a student be given notice, representation by legal counsel, and right to question witnesses against the pupil. Connecticut (1975)[14] passed an act concerning exclusion from school for disciplinary purposes. The legislation provides that no students shall be expelled without a formal hearing comporting with due process. The statute also provides for "alternative educational opportunity" for any expelled student and annual notice of board policies governing student conduct to all students. However, not all states have adopted "due process" procedures.

Once the requirements of the state statutes are known, the second step is to determine the requirements imposed by the state and federal constitutions. The most important procedure is the requirement of the Fourteenth Amendment to the U. S. Constitution that no person shall be deprived of "life, liberty, or property without due process of law." The next step is to determine what due process means with respect to student suspension and expulsion.

THE DIFFERENCE BETWEEN SUSPENSION AND EXPULSION: Suspension is normally considered to involve the exclusion of a pupil from a school for a brief, definite period of time (usually three to ten days), while expulsion usually denotes the exclusion of the students for a definite, extended period of time, the remainder of the school year.

The courts have ruled that due process, unlike some legal rules, is not a technical conception with a fixed content unrelated to

---

[13]Minnesota, General Statute 127.30 (1974).
[14]Connecticut General Statute Ann. 4 (c) 1975.

time, place, and circumstances. It is compounded of history, reason, the past course of decisions.[15] In essence, in any given instance, it must be judicially determined if school rules and regulations are fair and reasonable, if they have been applied in a fair and reasonable manner.[16]

Because of the due process requirements, educational decisions henceforth will have to be child-centered, a departure from the past, when educational decisions were more likely to require the child to fit the system. In addition, the due process requirements are likely to require educators to weigh the advisability of a particular "action" more carefully. Finally, due process serves to hold educators accountable to a child for a host of decisions.[17]

Due Process Cases

The earliest emphasis on procedural due process in secondary disciplinary cases seems to be a logical extension of judicial concern for the constitutional rights of students; this concern for the rights of students has been expressed in three important legal decisions. A landmark decision in secondary education was handed down in *Tinker v. Des Moines School District*,[18] in higher education in *Dixon v. Alabama State Board of Education*,[19] while the particular elements that constitute due process in a juvenile delinquency hearing was the subject of the decision *in re Gault*.[20]

In the first case, the petitioner John F. Tinker, fifteen years old, and petitioner Christopher Eckhardt, sixteen years old, attended high schools in Des Moines, Iowa. Petitioner Mary Beth Tinker, John's sister, was a thirteen-year-old student in junior high school.

In December 1965, a group of adults and students in Des Moines, Iowa held a meeting at the Eckhardt home. The group agreed to publicize their objections to the hostilities in Vietnam and their support for a truce by wearing black armbands during

---

[15]Knight v. State Board of Education, 200 F. Supp. 174 (M.D., Tenn. 1961).

[16]Wassow v. Trowbridge, 382 F.2d 807, 812 (2d Cir. 1967).

[17]*Contemporary Legal Problems in Education.* Topeka, Kansas: NOLPE, 1975, p. 193.

[18]Tinker v. Des Moines Independent Community School District, 393 U.S. 503, 49 Ohio op(2s) 222, 21 L. Ed. 2s 731, 89 Sup.Ct. 733 (1969).

[19]294 F. 2d 150 (Fifth Cir. 1961), *cert. denied*, 368 U.S. 930, L. Ed. 2d 193, 82 Sup.Ct. 368 (1961). Cast No. 23, *infra.* p. 183.

[20]387 U.S. 1, 40 Ohio op(2s) 387, 18 L. Ed. 2s 527, 87 Sup.Ct. 1428 (1967).

the holiday season and by fasting on December 16 and New Year's Eve.

The principals of the Des Moines schools became aware of the plan to wear armbands. On December 14, 1965, they met and adopted a policy that any student wearing an armband to school would be suspended until he returned without the armband. Petitioners were aware of the regulation that the school authorities adopted.

On December 16, Mary Beth and Christopher wore black armbands to their schools. John Tinker wore his armband the next day. They were all sent home and suspended from school until they came back without their armbands. They did not return to school until after the planned period for wearing armbands had expired—that is, until after New Year's Day. This complaint was filed in the United States District Court by petitioners, through their fathers, under 1983 of Title 42 of the U.S. Code. It prayed for an injunction restraining the defendant school officials and the defendant members of the board of directors of the school district from disciplining the petitioners, and it sought nominal damages.

The court found that students are "persons" under the Constitution and thus have fundamental rights that the state must respect. It found the wearing of black armbands to protest the Vietnam War to be such a right; the act was symbolic speech protected by the First Amendment.

Recognizing the state's important interest in protecting the orderly education of its children, the court affirmed the need for "comprehensive authority of the states and of school officials, consistent with fundamental safeguards, to prescribe and control conduct in the school." However, the court found that when the First Amendment rights of students and the rules of school officials collide, these two interests must be balanced to determine on the facts whether abridgement of student speech is justified.

The court concluded that the school regulation was an attempt to avoid controversy that might result from opposition to the Vietnam War shown by armbands. The schools are not a place where controversy can be eliminated, the court said, and in the absence of evidence that the wearing of armbands would "materially and substantially disrupt the work and discipline of the school," the school cannot prohibit such protest. The court made little attempt to clarify, define, or narrow the meaning of "material and substantial disruption."

In another case, *Burnside v. Byars*,[21] a number of high school students were suspended for wearing to school buttons that bore the legends "one man one vote" and "SNCC" after being warned by the principal that school regulations forbade such action. The evidence indicated that the school regulations forbade such action. The evidence indicated that the buttons evoked only "mild curiosity" from the school children. The court said this evidence was not basis for finding "material and substantial interference with the requirements of appropriate discipline in the operation of the school," a standard the court required to justify the abridgement of free speech. Thus, the Fifth Circuit found the wearing of "freedom buttons" to be protected "symbolic speech" and ordered the students reinstated.[22]

In another case, a board in New York State had a regulation prohibiting the wearing of slacks by girls except when permitted by the principal. A girl was suspended for violating the rule and sought injunction in court. The board's defense was made upon allegations of disruption or distraction, and rested on the general contention that the board was acting within its powers. The court held otherwise. It ruled that the board had not made the case for the dress code regulation. A regulation against wearing bell-bottom slacks by students, male or female, who ride bicycles to school can probably be justified in the interest of safety; so can, in the interest of discipline, a regulation against slacks that are so skintight and therefore revealing so as to provoke or distract students of the opposite sex; and in the interest of order, a regulation against slacks at the bottoms of which small bells have been attached. In other words, there must be a reason; the board could not get off with merely asserting its right to regulate slacks for girls without at the same time giving its reasons for attempting to limit individual rights in the service of a larger interest to be protected. To do so amounted in effect to denial of due process of law.[23]

---

[21]363 F.2d 744 (Fifth Cir. 1966).

[22]Aquirre v. Tohoka Independent School District, 311 F. Supp. 664 (N.D. Tex., 1970).

[23]Nolte, M. Chester: "Due Process: Where It's Taking Boards and How Yours Can Get There Safely." *The American School Board Journal.* pp. 34-36, Dec. 1971.

In an effort to define "substantial disruption", the Ninth Circuit Court ruled in *Karp v. Becker*. In this case, secondary officials cancelled an athletic award ceremony because they feared violent confrontation between students who had announced to the media that they planned to protest the school's nonrenewal of a teacher's contract and members of the school's athletic club who had threatened to prevent the protest.

Even though the ceremony was cancelled, some protesting students staged a walkout from classes. During the lunch hour, students and newsmen gathered in the school; the plaintiff (Karp) distributed signs supporting the teacher. The vice-principal asked the students to surrender the signs to him. All did except the plaintiff, who asserted that his right to possess and distribute the signs was protected by the First Amendment. After the second refusal, Karp surrendered the signs and was taken to the principal's office; chanting, pushing, and general disruption developed between the protestors and some members of the athletic club. School officials were successful in quelling the disturbance.

Karp was suspended for five days for bringing the signs on campus and distributing them to other students. In federal district court, he sought to enjoin permanently the enforcement of this suspension. The court ruled in favor of the school officials.[24]

Subsequent decisions based upon the Tinker ruling held that (1) a threat of disruption alone is insufficient reason to abridge student rights,[25] (2) rules must be relevant to the education function,[26] (3) the school may not discriminate in admission policy,[27] (4) rules must apply equally to female students,[28] (5) denial of a public education may not be arbitrary,[29] (6) regulations must be both preexisting and specific,[30] and (7) conduct may

---

[24]Karp. v. Becker, 477 F.2d 171 (Ninth Cir. 1973).

[25]Westley v. Rossi, 305 F. Supp. 706 (Minn. 1969); *Frontiers of School Law*, Topeka, Kansas: NOLPE, 1973, p. 181.

[26]Burnside v. Byars, 563 F.2d 744 (Miss. 1966; *supra* note 25, *Frontiers of School Law*.

[27]Burnside v. Byars, 231 F. Supp. 743 (Ala. 1964); *supra* note 25, *Frontiers of School Law*.

[28]Cash v. Hock, 309 F. Supp. 346 (Wis. 1970); *supra* note 25, *Frontiers of School Law*.

[29]Black v. Cothren, 316 F. Supp. 468 (Neb. 1970).

[30]Crossen v. Fatsi, 309 F. Supp. 702 (Wis. 1969).

not be repressed because of administrative personal disapproval.

The courts of this nation are not eager to take away power or limit the educational process. The Federal District Court for the Western District of Missouri, *En Banc* has stated:

> There have been, and no doubt in the future there will be, instances of erroneous and unwise misuse of power by those invested with powers of management and teaching the academic community, as in the case of all human affable institutions. When such misuse of power is threatened or occurs, our political and social order has made available a wide variety of lawful, nonviolent, political, economic and social means available to correct an unwise, but lawful choice of educational policy or action by those with the powers of management and teaching in the academic community. Only where the erroneous and unwise actions in the field of education deprive students of federally protected rights or privileges does a federal court have power to intervene in the educational process.[32]

Tinker as a Precedent

The Tinker ruling marked the watershed in student rights.

> The ruling sentiments of Tinker are found liberally sprinkled throughout many later court decisions. Surely no greater watershed case can be imagined in the field of school law than can Tinker which completely transformed students from objects of public direction to persons in their own right. That momentous change alone has made school administration and policy making very different from what was the case just five years ago.[33]

Based on the historical Tinker, the Supreme Court agreed with a Wisconsin farmer that his son need not attend public school beyond the eighth grade although state law required him to continue until the age of sixteen. A Pennsylvania federal judge permitted a parent to veto corporal punishment for her son in

---

[32]Becker, William H., John W. Oliver, William R. Collinson, and Elmo B. Hunter: "A Judicial Document on Student Discipline." *Educational Record*, Vol. 50, p. 17, Winter 1969.

[33]Nolte, M. Chester: "Brush Up in One Short Sitting: Ten Years of Tumult in School Law and Their Lessons." *The American School Journal*, p. 50, January 1974.

school. An Ohio federal judge refused to enforce a school board rule excluding a senior honor student from baseball eligibility because he was married. In other cases, boards were precluded from extending a suspension on top of another, from reducing grades as punishment, and from taking back a student's athletic letter as punishment for drinking beer. These cases were decided in favor of the plaintiffs based upon First Amendment rights being violated.

First Amendment Considerations

The First Amendment addresses such student activities as the distribution of underground newspapers, protest marches, picketing, and demonstrations.

The central questions for courts to answer is "When and to what degree do these behaviors constitute disruption to the educative processes?" Courts have found authority for prohibiting disruptive behavior citing *Tinker v. Des Moines Independent Community School District*,[34] in which the Supreme Court said, "conduct by the students which for any reason—whether it stems from time, place, or type of behavior—materially disrupts classwork or involves substantial disorder or invasion of the rights of others is, of course, not immunized by the constitutional guarantee of freedom of speech." The issue in Tinker involved conduct in school, but the clear implication was that First Amendment protections for students extend beyond the confines of school grounds and activities.

In determining whether a board of education or school administrators can limit potential disruption based on "reasonable forecast," the Fifth Circuit Court again applied the "reasonable forecast" standard of Tinker. It said that schools are not required to wait for a substantial disruption; they may act when officials can "reasonably forecast" disruption from free speech activity. In establishing the reasonable forecast standard, the court warned that mere administrative intuition is not enough; rather, objective evidence must support any forecast of disruption. The court concluded, "that balancing expression and

---

[34]Tinker v. Des Moines Independent Community School District, 393 U.S. 503, 49 Ohio op.(2d) 222, 21 L.Ed.2d 731, 89 Sup.Ct. 733 (1969).

discipline is a question of judgment for school administrators and boards and is subject only to the constitutional requirement of reasonableness under the circumstances."

The following cases are cited to illustrate First Amendment rights and reasonable forecast standards.

A federal district court in California upheld the suspension of students for distributing to other students just outside the school gates a paper that the school found to be vulgar and profane.[35] The court also held that when the bounds of decency are violated in publications distributed to high school students, whether on or off campus, the offenders become subject to discipline. The court applied the material and substantial disruption test and held that conduct "which has a tendency to impair the authority of teachers and to bring them into ridicule and contempt," as the underground newspaper apparently did from evidence presented, passes the test. The students argued that all their activity was off school grounds, but the court held that school authorities are responsible for morals of students while going to and from school as well as while on the premises.

In Tennessee, a student was suspended and later expelled for picketing in front of the school and "enticing students not to enter the building."[36] The conduct occurred during wide-spread boycotts of the city schools, which were causing a substantial disruption of the school program. The court held that while the original brief suspension of the student was lawful and indeed could have been expected in view of the repeated absences and picketing, the subsequent expulsion was not lawful. The court cited a failure of proof that the student in any way "incited students not to enter the building."

The courts have consistently held that schools by their very nature must encourage free inquiry and free expression of ideas. Such expression should include the personal opinion of students relevant to subject matter being taught, to school activities and policies, to school administration, and to matters of broad social concern and interest. However, in so expressing themselves, students must maintain the responsibility to refrain from the use of slanderous remarks, obscene language and materials, and substantive disruption.

---

[35]Baker v. Downey Board of Education, 307 F. Supp. 517 (C.D. Calif., 1969).
[36]Hobson v. Bailey, 309 F. Supp. 1593 (W.D. Tenn, 1970).

Just as students maintain the right to express their opinions freely by means of speech, so also do they maintain the right to express themselves freely by means of publications. Within the scope of expression itself, students maintain the responsibility to refrain from libel, obscenity, and irresponsible personal attacks. Within the scope of what is done with instruments of written expression—pamphlets, letters, newspapers, announcements, etc.—students have the responsibility to abide by reasonable rules and regulations established by boards of education, and implemented by school administrators. Furthermore, students who write, edit, publish, or distribute handwritten, printed, or duplicated material among their fellow students within the schools must assume full responsibility for the content of such material.[37]

Freedom of Assembly

Along with guaranteeing citizens the right to freedom of speech, the First Amendment guarantees the right to assemble peacefully, which is made applicable to the states by the Fourteenth Amendment; the Fourteenth Amendment guarantees life, liberty, and the pursuit of happiness, and the guarantee of due process of law; and the invasion of the right of parental control.

Along with the rights guaranteed by the Constitution, the right of individual citizens to assemble peacefully is subject to careful restrictions by school boards and enforced by school administrators.

Most of the cases dealing with assembly concern the freedom to belong to societies and fraternities.

The existence of secret organizations is a problem that school officials have been concerned with for decades. As early as 1912, a state appellate court in Illinois upheld action of the local school board of education in dismissing a student who belonged to a fraternity in violation of a board rule prohibiting such membership.[38] The validity of state statutes[39] and school board regulations

---

[37]*Rights and Responsibilities: Administrative Guidelines.* Columbus, Ohio: Division of Urban Education, Ohio Department of Education, 1971, p. 4.

[38]Smith v. Board of Education, 182 Ill.App. 342 (1912).

[39]Robinson v. Sacramento City Unified School District, 245 Cal.App.2d 278, 53 Cal.Rptr. 781, 788 (1966).

prohibiting secret organizations has been challenged often in succeeding years, but with one exception has been upheld consistently by the courts. The lone exception to the general rule occurred in Missouri.[40] In this instance, a local board attempted to regulate fraternity membership by banning members from participating in extracurricular activities and graduation exercises. The state supreme court refused to uphold the ruling of the local board and perpetually enjoined the board from enforcing it.

In deciding against students' rights to belong to societies or fraternities, the courts have recognized the importance of the right of freedom of assembly, but they distinguish between the rights of an adult and an adolescent. The court states it is not asserting that public school secondary students have no rights; yet, it reasons, since the students are adolescents in their formative years, they do not have the constitutional right of freedom of assembly in relation to joining a fraternity or sorority.

Dress Codes

School systems may not regulate a student's manner of dress unless they can show that the regulation is necessary to the performance of the school's educational mission. School dress policies that prohibit the wearing of pants by girls,[41] dungarees or jeans,[42] or any other general style of clothing[43] have been found to be impermissibly overbroad and unnecessary to prevent disruption and promote academic achievement.[44]

Schools may prohibit unsanitary, obscene, scanty, and suggestive clothing[45] and "a certain degree of arbitrariness will be tolerated to permit effective and speedy enforcement of such regulations."[46] In addition, health and safety considerations may empower schools to require that students wear certain clothing when participating in specific activities—swimming, hair nets in serving food, etc.

---

[40]Wright v. Board of Education of St. Louis, 295 Mo. 466, 246 S.W. 43 (1922).
[41]Johnson v. Joint School District No. 60, 95 Idaho 317, 508 P.2d 547 (1973).
[42]Wallace v. Ford, 346 F.2d 156 (E.D. Ark., 1972).
[43]Wallace v. Ford, 346 F.2d 156 (E.D. Ark., 1972).
[44]Miller v. Gillis, 315 F. Supp. 94 (N.D. Ill. 1969).
[45]Graber v. Kniola, 52 Mich.App. 269, 216 N.W.2d 925, 926 (1974).
[46]Wallace v. Ford, 346 F. Supp. 156, 163-64 (E.D. Ark., 1972).

Search and Seizure

Being "persons" under the constitution of the United States, students are protected from unreasonable search and seizure by either federal or state officials, including school officials. The problem faced in determining whether or not a school official may search either a student's person or those closed areas, such as lockers, in which students place personal items is directly analogous to the problems faced in determining the school official's role in regulating student appearance. A determination must be made of the point at which the student's right to protection against unreasonable search and seizure meets the school official's duty to act in such a manner as to carry out his statutory obligations to maintain an orderly and efficient school building and system.[47]

In the past, the school's right to search a student's person, his locker, or his car parked on school property had very seldom been questioned, because school officials had been considered private, not governmental, persons, whereas the Fourth Amendment's prohibition against unreasonable searches and seizures applied only to seizures by governmental officials.[48] Public school officials were considered, at one time, government employees. Some state courts have concluded that school officials are not the type of government officials restrained by the Fourth Amendment, or that when the official searches a student, he is acting *in loco parentis* and therefore assuming the private role of the parent to the student.[49]

Thus, the Fourth Amendment's usual requirements of probable cause and a search warrant have been held unnecessary for school searches and the exclusionary rule inapplicable to evidence discovered and seized by school officials during these searches. In recent years, however, courts have generally rejected the arguments that school officials are private persons for Fourth Amendment purposes.[50] They have begun to recognize that the Fourth Amendment's prohibition against unreasonable searches and seizures applies to searches by school officials.

---

[47]*Supra* note 37, p. 21.
[48]State v. Ward, 62 Mich.App. 46, 233 N.W.2d 180 (1975).
[49]Mercer v. State, 450 S.W.2d 715 (Tex. Ct. App. 1970.)
[50]State v. Young, 234 Ga. 488, 216 S.E.2d 586, *cert. denied*, 423 U.S. 1039 (1975).

The Fourth Amendment's prohibition against unreasonable searches has generally been construed to permit a search only when (1) the person whose interests are involved consents voluntarily,[51] (2) there is a probable cause to search and a warrant has been issued authorizing it, (3) there is probable cause and exigent circumstances such that taking time to obtain a warrant would frustrate the purpose of the search, or (4) a valid arrest has been made and a search is incidental to the arrest. When a search is made that does not comply with these requirements, four consequences may result: (1) criminal prosecution may be brought for violation of privacy,[52] (2) civil suit may be brought for violation of privacy,[53] (3) the evidence may be declared inadmissible in a school proceeding, or (4) the evidence may be inadmissible in a criminal proceeding.

Of these possible consequences, only the fourth is usually an issue. For example, no case has been found in which school officials have been criminally prosecuted for violating a student's privacy because of a search. Civil liability has been found in a few cases, however.[54]

In 1973, a federal district court in Pennsylvania ruled that a civil suit against school and police officials brought by nine high school students seeking damages for deprivation of their Fourth Amendment rights should proceed to trial.[55] In this case, school officials looking for a ring reported missing by another student requested police assistance after no student in the class in which the ring was first discovered missing came forward with it. The police made a strip search of the nine female students in the class but found no ring. The court held that, though the search had been conducted by the police, if it could be shown that school officials participated with the police in making statements and taking actions that coerced the students into submitting to the search, they could be held personally liable. The court overruled the defendant school official's motion to dismiss for failure to state a cause of action and ordered the case to be brought to trial.

---

[51]Commonwealth v. Dixon, 226 Pa. Super. 569, 323 A.2d 55 (1974).
[52]18 U.S.C. 242.
[53]Wood v. Strickland, 420 U.S. 565 (1975).
[54]Marlar v. Bell, 181 Tenn. 100, 178 S.W.2d 634 (1944).
[55]Potts v. Wright, 357 F.Supp. 215 (E.D. Pa., 1973).

A similar yet distinguishing factual situation presented itself in 1944, *Marlar v. Bill.*[56] Here a student was searched by a teacher to ascertain whether or not a dime had been stolen. The teacher alleged that her primary reason for searching the boy was to vindicate him from both the charge and suspicion of having stolen the dime. The Supreme Court of Tennessee agreed and held that the teacher stands in a somewhat limited sense *in loco parentis,* and may exercise such power of control as may be reasonably necessary.[57]

In another case,[58] a teacher searched a student who was suspected of having stolen money from another student. The student brought action to recover damages for trespass as a result of the forcible search of her person. The trial court directed a verdict in favor of the teacher, holding, among other things, "that a school teacher stands *in loco parentis,* and when a child is charged with taking money the teacher has a right to search the child the same as a parent would have in order to remove suspicion." The court also declared that a teacher only has those powers necessary to educate the student and to preserve order. Additionally, the appellate court reinforced the legal principle that a search warrant was not available to a private citizen.

Searches by School Officials

When searches have been conducted primarily by school officials in furtherance of school purposes, courts have found that the Fourth Amendment requires a less stringent standard to justify school searches of students and their property. Balancing the rights of students to be free from unreasonable searches and seizures with the compelling interest of the state in maintaining discipline and order in the public school system, most courts have concluded that items seized by school officials without a search warrant may be introduced in a criminal trial if the school official can show, at the time of the search, the existence of a "reasonable suspicion" that students were violating school regulations or

---

[56]Marlar v. Bell, 181 Tenn. 100, 178 S.W.2d 634 (1944).
[57]Marlar v. Bell, 181 Tenn. 100, 178 S.W.2d 634 (1944).
[58]12 Tenn. App. 354 (1930).

state laws. Reasonable suspicion is the standard generally applied to stop-and-frisk searches that are made without a warrant and are based on less than probable cause.

Weighing the Fourth Amendment rights of students against the state's interest in the school official who stands *in loco parentis*, one court concluded: "The *in loco parentis* doctrine is so compelling in light of public necessity and as a social concept antedating the Fourth Amendment, that any action, including a search taken thereunder upon reasonable suspicion, should be accepted as necessary and reasonable."[59] The courts have not been explicit in setting out what facts would justify a "reasonable suspicion." However, they have indicated that the state laws and the doctrine of *in loco parentis* impose on school officials an affirmative duty to investigate any situation where they are suspicious that conduct is occurring or materials are being harbored that would be dangerous or harmful to the health and welfare of students. This affirmative obligation to investigate grows out of the reasonable expectations of parents that the school will protect their children from dangerous conditions such as possession and sale of drugs or the possession of dangerous weapons by other students.

Search of Student Lockers

The Fourth Amendment protects an individual against unreasonable and illegal search by governmental officials. However, when lockers are searched the courts have stated that two requirements must be met: (1) the search must be within the scope of the school's duties, and (2) the search must be reasonable under the facts and circumstances.

In California, a vice-principal made a search of a locker without either the student's consent or the use of a warrant.[60] He did this after advising another student to make a purchase of drugs from the student maintaining the locker. The purchase was made, and when the locker was searched, four half cigarettes of marijuana and a plastic bag containing marijuana were found. As a result of this evidence, the student seller was subsequently

---

[59]Nelson v. State, 319 So.2d 154 (Fla. App. 1975).
[60]*In re* Donaldson, 269 Cal. App.2d 509, 75 Cal. Rptr. 220 (1969).

found in violation of the state's health and safety code. An appellate court, in affirming a lower court judgment, upheld the actions of the vice-principal.

In its decision, the court held that school officials have a responsibility for maintaining order on the school grounds, especially when the health and physical development of students are involved. The vice-principal was considered to be a private person by the court and not an agent of the state or other governmental unit; therefore, the Fourth Amendment protection against unreasonable searches did not come into play.

In another case, the Kansas Supreme Court upheld a burglary conviction based on the discovery of stolen goods in a bus station locker that was entered by a key removed from the defendant's locker.[61] The defendant had consented to the principal opening his school locker in the presence of the police. The court upheld the search on the basis of the defendant's uncoerced consent and the nature of the school locker.

When the search is conducted jointly by school officials and law enforcement agencies, the Fourth Amendment standards applicable usually depend on who initiated the search and place searched. When school officials, seeking to maintain order and to determine whether a school regulation or criminal statute has been violated, have regulated police assistance in conducting a search, the lesser reasonable suspicion standard has usually been applied.[62] When the search of a student or his property is initiated by the police and conducted jointly by school officials and law enforcement agents for the primary purpose of discovering evidence of a crime, the trend has been to hold that search and seizure standards applicable in criminal cases must be met.

Police-School Cooperation

A school principal may exercise his discretion in determining whether to request assistance of police in investigating a crime, or allegation of a crime, committed in his school building or school grounds during school hours. If a school principal requests assistance, a police officer may conduct a general investigation

---

[61]State v. Stein, 203 Kansas 638, 456 P.2d 1 (1969).
[62]Fred C., 26 Cal. App.3d 320, 102 Cal. Rptr. 682 (1972).

within the school building and interview students as possible *witnesses* in school during the day. The school principal or his designee should be present during the interview.

If a school principal has requested assistance by a police department to investigate a crime involving his school building or his students, the police should have permission to interrogate a student *suspect* in school during school hours. The school principal or the police should first notify the parents of the student of the intended interrogation. The school principal or his designee shall be present during the interrogation. If the interrogation by police is at the request of the school principal for the purpose of enforcing school discipline, or because the health and safety of the student or student body is involved, or because of the presence in school buildings or grounds of illegal matter, the police may interrogate the student without giving the student constitutional warnings. Although efforts should be made to notify the parents of the student, interrogation may proceed if the parent is unavailable or unwilling to attend.

If public health or safety is involved, upon request of a school principal who should be present, police officers may make a general search for drugs, weapons, or items of an illegal or prohibited nature in students' lockers and desks, or students' or non-students' cars. If a principal has received reliable information, which he believes to be true, that evidence of a crime or stolen goods not involving school property of members of the school staff or student body is located in a certain student's locker, desk, or automobile, and search is unrelated to school discipline or health and safety of a student or the student body, he should request police assistance and procedures to obtain and execute a search warrant.

Police officers may not search students' lockers, desks, or automobiles unless they have a search warrant and may not search a student's person in school unless the student is under arrest. A school official may not consent to a warrantless search of a student's locker, desk, or automobile.

Administrative Guidelines[63]

1. When it appears absolutely necessary to prevent imminent

---

[63]*Supra* note 37, pp. 22-23.

harm either to a student himself or to others, a student may be restrained or searched.

2. When there is clear reason to believe that a student has on his person a dangerous and illegal item and that there is imminent danger of harm because of such possession, school officials may take any reasonable steps necessary to prevent such harm.

3. Systematic secretive searches of student lockers or other closed areas wherein the students may keep personal items should most unqualifiedly *not take place.*

4. When there is clear reason to believe that a dangerous and illegal item is secreted in a purse, satchel, briefcase, or any other container used by students for the purpose of of carrying personal items and that there is imminent danger of harm either to the student or to others if the student retains possession of that item, seizure of the container in which is believed to be secreted shall not be construed as being unreasonable or violative of the student's rights under the Fourth and Fourteenth Amendments of the United States Constitution.

5. If there is clear reason to believe that an automobile used by a student as transportation to and from school contains a dangerous and illegal item, parents of the student operating the automobile should be contacted immediately and asked to take responsibility for removing the automobile from school grounds. Where this is impractical or impossible, proper authorities should be contacted and a search warrant obtained. Where there is a clear reason to believe that there will be imminent danger, either to the student himself, or to others, should the student come into possession of the item, the student should be detained until either parents or authorities or both arrive.

Hair Codes

The most frequently litigated issue in student appearance cases concerns the regulation of hair length on male students. Five of the ten circuits of the United States Courts of Appeals (First, Third, Fourth, Seventh, and Eighth) have ruled that students have a constitutionally protected right to choose their own hair style,[64] and this right extends to all school activities

---

[64]Massie v. Henry, 455 F.2d 779 (Fourth Cir. 1972); Richards v. Thurston, 424 F.2d 1281 (First Cir. 1970).

including athletics.[65] However, these five circuits have not agreed on the constitutional basis of this right.

The First Amendment's guarantee of free expression,[66] the Ninth Amendment's guarantee of the right of privacy,[67] and the Fourteenth Amendment's guarantee of due process and equal protection[68] have all been used to provide the constitutional underpinning for the right of male students to wear long hair.[69] While this right is not absolute, it has sufficient constitutional magnitude for these courts to require school systems to meet a substantial burden of justification to regulate student hairstyles.

The following cases are cited to illustrate the rulings by various courts concerning hairstyle litigation. A United States District Court in Georgia has upheld the right of the administration to require male students to shave their mustaches.[70] The judges went further to say administrators should be free to establish and enforce rules and regulations designed to foster "appropriate" school conduct.

Another case dealing with grooming regulations pertaining to extracurricular activities (band) was decided in a federal district court in Arkansas.[71] The court decided against a twelve-year-old seventh-grade public school student who had been dismissed from band because of his wearing long hair. In upholding the school policy, the court stated:

> A public school band is a group within a group. Like any other military or concert band it is characterized by regimentation, and except in a specialist category, it has no place for an individual exhibitionist.[72]

Consequently, the court contended it was not unreasonable for the school to require that the length and arrangement of hair of either sex correspond to "generally accepted norms of appearance."

In Westley v. Rossi,[73] a federal court in Minnesota held that the

---

[65]Long v. Zopp, 476 F.2d 180 (Fourth Cir. 1973).

[66]Breen v. Kahl, 419 F.2d 1034 (Seventh Cir. 1969).

[67]Breen v. Kahl, 419 F.2d 1034 (Seventh Cir., 1969).

[68]Stull v. School Board, 459 F.2d 339 (Third Cir. 1972).

[69]Olff v. East Side Union High School District, 445F.2d 932 (Ninth Cir. 1971).

[70]Stevenson v. Wheeler County Board of Education, 306 F. Supp. 97 (S.D. Ga., 1969).

[71]Corley v. Daunhauer, 312 F. Supp. 811 (E.D. Ark., 1970).

[72]Corley v. Daunhauer, 312 F. Supp. 817 (E.D. Ark., 1970).

[73]305 F. Supp. 706 (Minn. 1969).

student's constitutional rights were violated when he was required to obtain a "neat, conventional" haircut. The court gave several reasons for its holding. The court opined that no health hazard existed if hair was long and uncombed, as long as it was clean. There was no evidence that material and substantial disruption occurred, since the student's suspension made it impossible empirically to determine this. The court also held that a regulation must have a reasonable relationship to the school curriculum or to the carrying out of the school's responsibility.

When formulating standards regarding hair styles, the key legal question is usually pointed toward arbitrary infringement upon the constitutionally protected rights of other individual human beings. Such infringement is permissible only to the extent that the wearing of long hair substantially disrupts the educational process and prevents the board from carrying out its statutory obligations.

Rights of Married Students

Permanent exclusion of students because they have or will soon have children has been found impermissible in light of strong state policies encouraging the education of children.[74] School rules and regulations in some instances have not attempted to bar married students from school completely; rather, they have attempted to suspend the student. These kinds of regulations, with one exception, have not been upheld by the appellate courts. Temporary exclusion from or restriction on school attendance based on parental status has been approved by a few courts. In Ohio,[75] a regulation requiring a pregnant student to withdraw from school as soon as she learns she is pregnant was found to be proper and wise to protect her health, safety, and well-being from the "typical rough-and-tumble characteristics of children in high school." In this case, the school allowed the student to receive full credit by doing her assignments at home.

Most courts have found that excluding pregnant students from school or restricting their school activities is not permissible except when it is determined that an individual's health problems

---

[74]Alvin Independent School District v. Cooper, 404 S.W.2d 76 (Tex. Civ. App., 1966).
[75]State *ex rel.* Idle v. Chamberlain, 175 N.E.2d 539 (Ohio App., 1961).

justify such actions. The most objectionable aspect of excluding pregnant students is the element of sex discrimination: female students have been the primary recipients of this discipline. Congress has forbidden sex discrimination by recipients of federal educational funds.[76] The regulations enforcing this legislation expressly prohibit discrimination or exclusion of any student from a school's educational program, including extra-curricular activities, "on the basis of such student's pregnancy, miscarriage, abortion, or recovery therefrom." The only exceptions allowed under the legislation are when students voluntarily ask to be excused or their physicians certify that a different program is necessary for her physical or mental health. These regulations also require that schools recognize pregnancy as a valid reason for a reasonable level of absence, after which the student must be reinstated to her original status.

Challenges to board policies excluding pregnant students center upon the constitutional guarantees of the right of association, the right to privacy, and the right to due process and equal protection of the laws. The courts view exclusion from the public schools as a deprivation of a fundamental right. Although it is clearly established that school boards have the authority to promulgate policies controlling conduct of students, such policies cannot be capricious, arbitrary, or unreasonable. Common law decisions established that pregnant students and mothers, whether wed or unwed, had a constitutional right to due process.

The reasoning "that out-of-wedlock pregnancy was proof of immoral character, that teenage mothers posed a disruptive threat to school operations, and that pregnant students caused moral contamination of other students" were all struck down by the courts.

While lack of moral character has been recognized as a proper reason for excluding a child from public schools,[77] most recent court decisions find the fact that a student is an unwed mother to be insufficient by itself to justify exclusion.[78] Courts that would allow exclusion based on lack of moral character require that before the exclusion the unwed mother be given written notification of charges of immoral character—that her presence in the

---

[76]Title IX of the Ed. Amend. of 1972, 20 U.S.C.1681 (Supp., 1972).

[77]Perry v. Grenada, 300 F. Supp. 748, 753 (N.D. Miss., 1969).

[78]Ordway v. Hargraves, 323 F. Supp. 1115 (D. Mass., 1971).

public schools would taint the education of other students.[79]

In a case in Mississippi,[80] illustrating immoral character, the case was concerned with the exclusion from public school of two unwed mothers. The court held that the plaintiffs could not be excluded from the public schools for the sole reason that they were unwed mothers. The court went on to say that they were entitled to readmission unless on a fair hearing before school authorities they were found to be so lacking in moral character that their presence in the schools would taint the education of other students.

The Court of Appeals of Texas upheld a married student's right to attend school after she became a mother. In this instance, school board policy permitted married students without children to attend public schools but forbade the attendance of a married mother. Provisions of the rule, however, encouraged such students to continue their education in local adult education programs. Because of her age (sixteen) the student was not eligible to attend an adult program. The court held that, although local boards may pass rules they deem necessary to maintain, such a rule cannot, in effect, permanently exclude a person of scholastic age from attendance at a public school.[81]

The right of a student to an equal educational opportunity has now been legally established. Pregnant students as well as teenage mothers cannot be denied this constitutional right. School authorities must acknowledge this right and refrain from imposing upon students archaic standards of morality that violate their individual rights.

Due Process and the Schools

Due process, as has been mentioned, is perhaps the biggest issue facing school boards as a result of the student rights movement. The Supreme Court has suggested that each day in school is important to a child and denial of schooling for even a few days amounts to a denial of due process of law.

While suspension and expulsion of students from school may be a necessary and justifiable organizational response to a

---

[79]Shull v. Columbus Mun. Sep. School District, 338 F. Supp. 1376 (N.D. Miss., 1972).
[80]Perry v. Granada Mun. Sep. School District, 300 F. Supp. 748 (N.D. Miss., 1969).
[81]Alvin Independent School District v. Cooper, 404 S.W.2d 76 (Tex., 1966).

critical problem, the consequences of the action for the student render it imperative that the decision to exclude be substantively and procedurally fair. Increasingly, attention is being devoted to the question whether the exclusion of a student from school is compatible with the right to due process under the Fourteenth Amendment.[82]

School officials are finding that their actions of suspensions and/or expulsions for even a few days must be explainable not only to the board for which they work but to the courts as well. Today, board members must serve a dual capacity: a board member is, in the final analysis, not an exclusive agent of the state alone, but rather "a part-time advocate of the student." He cannot use the power of the state to deprive even the least of these or any of his constitutional rights, no matter how insignificant or petty. His role is now one of compassion for "persons" who otherwise may have not means of asserting a right to life, liberty, or the pursuit of happiness save through the board member's effort on his behalf.[83]

Throughout the country the application of the due process clause of the Fourteenth Amendment has changed the conditions of public school disciplinary actions. The overriding question is "Under what conditions is legal due process required in suspension and expulsion?" The courts have held that any type of legal action against a student must incorporate due process.

Due Process Requirements

The big question most school officials are facing is "How do we meet the requirements of due process"? This question has been addressed by seven authorities in the field of school law. Michael E. Manley-Casimir:

First, school authorities must specify both prescribed and proscribed conduct in a code of unambiguous rules. Vague or overly broad rules are often overturned by the courts on the grounds that they are unenforceable. Second, the school must furnish a written statement to the affected student and his parents specifying the charges, the nature of the evidence on

---

[82]*Supra* note 8, p. 1.
[83]Supra note 23, p. 36.

which the charges are based, the regulation involved, and the time and place of the hearing. Third, the school should permit a reasonable period of time between the notice and the hearing itself; that is to say, sufficient time for the student to prepare for the hearing. Fourth, the student must be informed of his rights before the hearing occurs.[84]

Robert E. Phay:

First, the school must forewarn the student of the type of conduct that if engaged in, will subject him to expulsion. Second, the school must present to the student accused of a violation and his parents a written statement specifying the charges against him and the nature of the evidence to support the charges on which the disciplinary procedure is based. Besides reciting the factual allegations against the student, the statement should refer to a specific rule or regulation that has been violated and state where the hearing is to be held.

Although prior notice of the hearing is an absolute requisite for due process, the school discharges its responsibility if it honestly attempts to reach the student and his parents by telephoning him and sending a registered letter to his home. If the student cannot be reached because he has changed his address or is deliberately avoiding notification, he cannot later complain that he did not receive notice.

Third, the school should allow the accused student some time to prepare for the hearing by scheduling it to take place several days after the student has been notified of the charges against him. Two days would probably be a minimum time between a notice and a hearing unless the student agreed to an immediate hearing. One court recently held that a high school student be given a minimum of five days' notice before a hearing on his expulsion.

Fourth, the school must inform the student of his procedural rights before a hearing. The requirement can be accomplished by sending him, at the time he is notified of the charges, a printed statement outlining the procedure. It is good practice for the school to include in its student handbook a complete disciplinary and procedural code. Sending the student a copy of the handbook should satisfy the aspect of notice.[85]

---

[84]*Supra* note 23, p. 4
[85]Supra note 12, pp. 22-23.

M. Chester Nolte:

Students may still be suspended or expelled, but not without due consideration being given to the fairness and good faith of the grounds and procedures to be employed by the board.

There must be no impermissible grounds used to suspend or expel students as well as no arbitrary procedure employed in the process. Both rules are essential elements of due process of law.

The nature of the hearing will depend upon the circumstances, but in general, will include a notice of reasons given, a confrontation with his accusers, and an opportunity given to be heard. The board cannot assert the opinion that it has taken the action being challenged simply because it has power to do so—it must be prepared to show disruption, health reasons, or other extenuating circumstances if called upon in court to do so.

The burden of proof of the validity of its procedures rests eventually with the board, on the federal requirement that, before the state or any of its subdivisions can limit an individual's rights, it must show overriding cause and larger public purpose to be served. Failure here means failure of the board's case in full.

The criterion throughout is fairness: Is it fair? If there is doubt about the answer, the board should consider itself in trouble.

Finally, students both in and out of school are "persons" under our Constitution. There cannot be one standard for them, another for adults. No double standard will survive. That which every father would want for his son—even that should he be prepared to supply for every mother's son in his school.[86]

C. A. Hollister:

1. The student shall be entitled to a hearing before the proper disciplinary body.
2. The student shall be further entitled to receive a statement in writing, at least two days prior to the hearing, setting forth the charges against him with sufficient clarity to enable him to present a reasonable defense thereto.
3. The student shall be further entitled to learn the names of the witnesses who are responsible for having reported the alleged violation. If there are no witnesses, the student shall be fully informed of the manner in which the alleged violation came to the attention of the disciplinary body.

---

[86]*Supra* note 23, p. 36.

4. The student should be entitled to present his defense to the disciplinary body while the members are gathered for the hearing, including the presentation by the student of a reasonable number of witnesses in his own behalf.
5. Should the student desire, he can be accompanied and represented by legal counsel or by a lay advisor.
6. The student shall be entitled to an expeditious handling of his case and prompt decisions after the hearing, consistent with the requirements of mature and careful reflection by the disciplinary body.
7. Lastly, the student shall be afforded an explicit explanation in writing of the basis for any decision rendered against him.[87]

Harry C. Mallios:

First, a student must be notified well in advance of a hearing exactly what he is charged with and, additionally, he must be given an opportunity to be heard.

Further, the student should be allowed the opportunity of being represented by someone designated by him such as parent or legal guardian, and if warranted, to ask questions of witnesses against him or have the right to call witnesses to appear for him. Then, upon hearing testimony from both sides, finding of fact is made based upon the evidence as presented by both sides. If the offense is of such a serious nature as to result in a major penalty being administered, such as exclusion from school, a record or transcript of the proceedings should be kept.

Finally, if the student is not afforded a fair hearing, in his opinion, he may have the right to appeal for a review.[88]

John Stephen, in his doctoral dissertation, found three major areas of court agreement in procedural due process:

1. Public school attendance carries with it certain rights which may not be disregarded by categorization of such attendance as a "privilege."
2. The law in the vast majority of the states concerning notice and some opportunity for a hearing prior to dismissal from the public schools is vague, incomplete, and productive of litigation.
3. The cases litigated thus far, resulting from the condition

---

[87]Hollister, *Op. Cit.*, p. 35.
[88]Mallios, *Op. Cit.*, p. 88.

of the state law in this area, demonstrate increased judicial interpretation of the Fourteenth Amendment to require notice and some opportunity for a hearing for pupils facing possible dismissal from the public school.[89]

The Federal District Court of Western Missouri answered:

First, the student should be given adequate notice in writing of the specific ground or grounds and the nature of the evidence on which the disciplinary proceedings are based. Second, the student should be given an opportunity for a hearing in which the disciplinary authority provides a fair opportunity for hearing the student's position, explanations, and evidence. The third requirement is that no disciplinary action can be taken on grounds which are not supported by adequate evidence.[90]

Although there is not complete agreement on the procedural process, most authors feel the following to be the major points of commonality:

1. The rules, regulations, and policies of the school should be common knowledge of the student body.
2. A written notice of the hearing should be given to the student. The hearing should take place after the student has had adequate time to prepare a defense and/or an explanation of the charges.
3. The student has the right to confront his accusers at the hearing.

It should be noted that courts still leave room for immediate suspension or expulsion in emergencies. Manley-Casimir gave the following explanation concerning such cases:

In situations where the continued presence of a particular student in school endangers his own or others' safety and well-being or where the student has knowingly violated a rule for which the specified penalty is suspension, the courts have upheld ten-day summary suspensions without the requisite notice of charges or a prior hearing on the case, as long as a hearing is held subsequently.[91]

---

[89]Stephen, John: "The Legal Status of Pupil Suspensions and Expulsions and Due Process." *Dissertation Abstracts International*, Series A, Vol. 31, p. 4437-A, 1971.

[90]*Supra* note 32, p. 15.

[91]*Supra* note 8, p. 3.

Summary

It is generally accepted today that high school students are entitled to due process when they are subjected to major disciplinary action such as suspension, expulsion, or any other action that will gravely affect their records, reputations, and future opportunities in society, particularly opportunities to pursue careers and obtain employment. "Due process" in the context of quasijudicial administrative proceedings carried out by school authorities does not mean that the procedures used by courts in juvenile proceedings must be followed exactly by school authorities when engaged in disciplinary proceedings. It does mean that clear, definite, and fundamentally fair rules of procedure must govern disciplinary action taken by school authorities. Such procedure is necessary to guarantee that a student will not be deprived of so fundamentally important a thing as a high school education or any substantial portion thereof, without substantial and just cause.

Compendium of Cases

I. High school students expelled for committing acts of assault and battery claim civil right of due process was denied them on several counts: first, that the notices of the expulsion hearings were defective because of failure to state student's right to be represented by counsel, to present evidence, and to confront and cross examine witnesses; second, that the legal counsel for the board also acted as prosecutor during the hearings creating a bias against the students; third, the school authorities acted improperly when allowing hearsay evidence at the hearings (identification by looking at yearbook pictures); fourth, that students' failure to testify in their own behalf (use of the First Amendment) was commented on as an admission of guilt.

Several important comments were made by the court in dismissing the charges against five of the students involved and upholding the board of education in the expulsion of five students. In a review of the evidence the court stated that clear and convincing proof of an act must be produced by the board in the denial of a student's right to attend a public school—the more serious the penalty "the more process that is due." The court further commented that the involvement of the superintendent of schools in the expulsion hearing made it more difficult for the board to act freely in the deliberation of the issues.[92]

II. A school board policy prohibiting married students from participating in extracurricular activities was held to be a denial of equal protection under the Fourteenth Amendment.[93]

III. Where the petitioner's son was beyond the age for compulsory attendance and was suspended by the board of education, ostensibly for reasons of continuous excessive absences over a period of several years, the district is under no legal obligation to continue to provide for his education.[94]

IV. The United States District Court in Virginia[95] ruled that a three-day suspension of a student was not *de minimis* so as to excuse school officials from adhering to the due process requirements spelled out by the United States Supreme Court.[96]

> A suspension is noted on a child's records, and these records are often used by potential employers and admissions personnel at colleges and universities. Any time a child misses his classes, he is deprived of a learning experience that cannot be repeated. This court is compelled to find that a three-day suspension is not *de minimus*; therefore, due process is required in the suspension of this plaintiff.

V. The school board had a rule prohibiting drinking by members of the high school basketball team with the penalty for violation to be immediate expulsion from the squad. All members of the team and their parents were informed of the rule. Members of both the girls' and boys' teams participated in a party where they drank alcoholic beverages. They admitted it, were suspended from the squad, and were informed they could have a hearing with counsel, witness, etc. The students and their parents did not participate in the hearing but went to the trial court for a temporary and permanent injunction on the grounds the rule was arbitrary and unreasonable and that their constitutional

---

[92]Gonzales v. McEuen, 435 F. Supp. 460 (D. Cal. 1977).
[93]Beeson v. Kiowa City School District, RE-1, 567 P.2d 801 (Colo. App. 1977).
[94]*In re* Kozer, 17 Educ. Dept. Rep., N.Y. Comm'r Dec. No. 9519 (1977).
[95]Hillman v. Elliott, 436 F. Supp. 812 (W.D. Va., 1977).
[96]Goss v. Lopez, 419 U.S. 565 (1975).

liberty and property rights were violated. The trial court granted the injunction. On appeal the Supreme Court reversed even though case was moot because the students had graduated. The Court held that a matter of public interest was involved. The rule was found to be reasonable and proper and that the flexible type due process required in the circumstances had been provided. No constitutional liberty or property right had been denied.[97]

VI. Petitioner's daughter was among a group of students who entered the high school building. It is also unrefuted that property was both stolen and damaged by this group of students. Patricia avers that she was not responsible for the theft or damage, but she does not deny that she entered the school building improperly and was present during the incident. The curtailment of extracurricular activities for the spring semester was held not to be an unreasonable penalty. However, the commissioner pointed out that it is not appropriate for the board to present its determination in the form of a recommendation to the assistant principal.[98]

---

[97]Braesch v. DePasquale, 265 N.W.2d 84 2d (Neb. 1978).
[98]*In re* Swain, 17 Educ. Dept. Rep., N.Y. Comm'r Dec. No. 9674 (1978).

Chapter 6

TEACHERS' CIVIL RIGHTS AND RESPONSIBILITIES

Since the early history of this country, the public has been far more restrictive in its expectations for the conduct of teachers than for the conduct of the average lay citizen. Beale cites incidents recorded during the mid-nineteenth century in which teachers were reprimanded, dismissed, fined, imprisoned, and subjected to mob harassment for real or imagined violations of prevailing public standards.[1] Such violations included teaching black students[2] and advocating abolition of slavery.[3]

A few decades ago it was a common practice to regulate all aspects of teachers' lives and to subject them to conditions of employment that violated their constitutional rights. The following provisions were not uncommon in teacher's contracts in the past:

1. I promise to take a vital interest in all phases of Sunday school work, donating my time, service, and money without stint for the uplift and benefit of the community.
2. I promise to abstain from all dancing, immodest dressing, and any other conduct unbecoming a teacher and lady.
3. I promise not to go out with any young men except insofar as it may be necessary to stimulate Sunday school work.
4. I promise not to fall in love, to become engaged or secretly married.
5. I promise not to encourage or tolerate the least familiarity

---

[1]Beale, H.: *A History of Freedom of Teaching in American Schools.* 1941, pp. 3-11.
[2]*Supra* note 1, p. 131.
[3]*Supra* note 1, pp. 143-156.

on the part of my boy pupils.

6. I promise to sleep at least eight hours a night, to eat carefully, and to take every precaution to keep in the best of health and spirits, in order that I may be better able to render efficient service to my pupils.

7. I promise to remember that I owe a duty to the townspeople who are paying me wages; that I owe respect to the school board and the superintendent that hired me; and that I shall consider myself at all times the willing servant of the school board and the townspeople.[4]

In 1900, state statutes contained provisions that prescribed the personal attributes required for teacher certification and what subjects could and could not be taught. In Arkansas, teachers were not certified "who did not believe in the Supreme Being, who were given to profanity, drunkenness, gambling, licentiousness or other demoralizing vices."[5]

During this period it was not uncommon for teachers to be dismissed for real or imagined conduct. In a 1939 study, Anderson found "in most states teacher dismissal was on a personal rather than a professional basis."[6] His conclusive summary of reasons for dismissal were: incompetency and inefficiency (34), reassignment and transfer (26), insubordination (24), marriage and childbirth (25), neglect of duty (22), abolition of position (21), abandonment of position (18), immorality (17), general unpopularity (8), unprofessional conduct (7), anticipated causes (6), and political activity (4).[7]

Bolmeier, in reviewing the communities' expectations of teacher's behavior, found in 1960 that "teachers were more restricted than most citizens in the exercise of their freedoms guaranteed by the Constitution."[8]

To sum up the public's expectations of teachers, Koening stated:

For the teacher who would avoid dismissal . . . guidelines

---

[4]Minehan, T.: "The Teacher Goes Job Hunting." *Nation,* 124: p. 606, May-June 1927.

[5]Elshee, *Op. Cit.,* p. 355.

[6]Anderson: *Trends in Causes of Teacher Dismissal as Shown by American Court Decision 9.* Ed.D. Dissertation, George Peabody College of Teachers, 1939.

[7]*Supra* note 6, pp. 5-6.

[8]Bolmeier, Edward C.: "Legal Scope of Teachers' Freedoms." *Education Forum,* 24, pp. 199-206, 1960.

[should] include the avoidance of illicit sexual activity; the avoidance of actions which might cast doubt on either character or reputation; a thorough knowledge of the community in which service is being performed; and a readiness to forfeit a certain degree of personal independence and freedom of action. . . .[9]

Today, many parents, administrators, and school board members still believe that local communities can and should control the behaviors of teachers. The controls they seek to impose, though less extreme than those at the beginning of the century, often lead to partial revocation of the Bill of Rights in the lives of teachers.

The Modern View

A public school teacher possesses certain rights and freedoms enjoyed by all citizens. As a citizen, s/he has the legal right to speak, think, and believe as s/he wishes. As a public school teacher, however, s/he must exercise these and other legal rights with due consideration of the effects upon others, particularly school children. By virtue of his/her position, performing a governmental function, s/he must conform to certain laws, rules, and regulations not equally applicable to the ordinary citizen.

All rights afforded the teacher have limitations. Even rights stipulated in the statutes and constitutions are not absolute. The rights may be exercised only under certain conditions such as determined by place, time, and manner. Generally, the courts will hold that the degree to which a teacher may exercise a right will depend upon the effect it would have upon pupils and the prevailing conditions in the community. Therefore, the purpose of this chapter is to cover the main issues concerning the teacher in which the limitations of teachers' civil rights are involved.

Academic Freedom

Academic freedom, as applied to teachers, denotes the right to teach subject matter within the professional competence of the

---

[9]Koening: "Teacher Immorality and Misconduct." *American School Board Journal,* 155, p. 19, 1968.

instructor without undue restraints or interferences from school administrators or other officials. The purpose of academic freedom is to create an atmosphere in which knowledge can be freely transmitted and the critical faculties of students can be developed through unfettered research and discussion. Academic freedoms are those freedoms guaranteed by the Bill of Rights of the Federal Constitution as elaborated by the courts.[10]

The courts have ruled: "Our nation is deeply committed to safeguarding academic freedom, which is of transcendent value to all of us and not merely to the teachers concerned. That freedom is therefore a special concern of the First Amendment, which does not tolerate laws that cast a pall of orthodoxy."[11] As further noted by the court: "First Amendment rights, applied in light of the special characteristics of the school environment, are available to teachers and students. Academic freedom can be equated with first amendment rights, leaving open only the question of the extent to which these rights can be exercised within the classroom."[12]

As with all constitutional rights, academic freedom is not absolute; it must be balanced against other competing public interests. The state, acting *in loco parentis*, has a compelling interest in the welfare of children and therefore may regulate teacher conduct in the classrooms. Such regulations, however, must meet certain standards before courts will uphold their validity.

In order for school officials to justify prohibition of a particular expression of academic freedom, they must be able to show that the denial was caused by something more than a mere desire to avoid the discomfort and unpleasantness that always accompanies an unpopular viewpoint, or to prevent material and substantial disruption to the educative process.

In an academic freedom case before the Supreme Court in 1937, Chief Justice Warren ruled "to impose an intellectual straight-jacket on our educational leaders would be to imperil the future of our nation."[13]

---

[10]Fuchs: "Academic Freedom—Its Basic Philosophy, Function, and History." *Law and Contemporary Problems,* 28, p. 431, 1963.
[11]Keyishian v. Board of Regents, 385 U.S. 589 (1967).
[12]Keyishian v. Board of Regents, 385 U.S. 603 (1967).
[13]Sweezy v. New Hampshire, 354 U.S. 234, 250 (1937).

Judicial protection of academic freedom is based on the First Amendment and on the belief that teachers and students should be free to question and challenge established concepts in a democratic society. Like other constitutional rights, however, academic freedom is not absolute. Hence courts use a "balancing test" to decide these cases: they balance the teacher's right of academic freedom against the competing interests of society in maintaining reasonable school discipline. Generally this means that a teacher's use of controversial material or language is protected by the First Amendment unless a school board can demonstrate that (1) it is not relevant to the subject being taught, (2) it is not appropriate to the age and maturity of the students, or (3) it substantially disrupts the educational process.

Recognizing, in some cases, the state may have a valid interest in regulating the speech of its employees, the Court commented that the proper inquiry "is to arrive at a balance between the interests of the teacher, as a citizen, in commenting upon matters of public concern, and the interests of the state, as an employer, in promoting the efficiency of the public and its services through its employees."[14]

The Court additionally considered the impact of the truth or falsity of the teacher's comment on the exercise of the constitutional privilege. The Court said that it could imagine situations where the school administration would have the right to limit a teacher's right to speak under certain conditions:

> It is possible to conceive of some positions in public employment in which the need for confidentiality is so great that even completely correct public statements might furnish a permissable ground for dismissal. Likewise, positions in public employment in which the relationship between supervisor and subordinate is of such a personal and intimate nature that certain forms of public criticism of the superior by the subordinate would seriously undermine the effectiveness of the working relationship between them can also be imagined.[15]

In this case, a board of education dismissed a teacher for writing and sending to a newspaper for publication a letter

---

[14]Pickering v. Board of Education, 391 U.S. 568 (1968).
[15]Pickering v. Board of Education, 319 U.S. 570, N.3 (1968).

criticizing the board's allocation of school funds between educational and athletic programs and the board's way of informing, or not informing, the public of the "real" reasons why additional tax revenues were being sought for schools. The dismissal resulted from a determination by the board, after a full hearing, that the publication of the letter was "detrimental to the efficient operation and administration of the schools of the district" and that, therefore, under the relevant Illinois statute, "the interest of the school required dismissal." Some of the statements in the teacher's letter were substantially true. Others were false, but seemed to be the product of faulty research rather than being knowingly, maliciously, or recklessly false. The teacher challenged the constitutionality of the dismissal. In this case, the dismissal of the teacher was held to be improper.

False Statements

As to false statements, the Court has applied a principle based on *New York Times Co. v. Sullivan.*[16] Under Sullivan, the court proceeded on the basis that if the right of free speech means anything, it must include the right to make false statements as well as true ones; in other words, the First Amendment permits one to be wrong in a public discussion. The only proviso is that the statements must not be known to be false or made recklessly.[17]

However, the Court noted that there might be some limitations on the right to make false statements even in good faith, if it could be shown that the statement "implied the teacher's proper performance of his daily duties in the classroom or . . . interfered with the regular operation of the schools generally."[18] The Court does not decide whether a statement that was knowingly or recklessly false would, if not proven to have harmful effects, still be protected by the First Amendment.

Freedom of Speech Outside the Classroom

The First Amendment was designed to protect the freedom of

---

[16]New York Times Co. v. Sullivan, 376 U.S. 254, 271 (1964).
[17]New York Times Co. v. Sullivan, 376 U.S. 254, 271 (1964).
[18]Pickering v. Board of Education, 391 U.S. 572-73 (1968).

citizens to speak or write critically about government policies and public officials. Whether the criticism is balanced or biased, careful or sloppy, it generally does not jeopardize an individual's job.[19] Exactly how far a teacher can go in the exercise of "freedom of speech" is not clear.

Until the 1950s, the constitutional right of free speech was found to be essentially irrelevant to the question of whether teachers could make public comments that displeased the administration of the public agency that employed them. Commenting on the rights and restrictions placed on teachers' freedom of speech, Justice Oliver Wendell Holmes stated:

> There are few employments for hire in which the servant does not agree to suspend his constitutional rights of free speech, as well as idleness, by the implied terms of his contract. The servant cannot complain, as he takes the employment on the terms which are offered to him.[20]

This ruling by Justice Holmes was simple. Public employment is something that no citizen can demand; it is a privilege that carries certain restrictions—written and unwritten. When these restrictions are violated and a public employee is discharged for exercising his right of free speech, no right has been violated since the employee had no "right" to public employment in the first place. Moreover, since he does not have to work for the government, his right to speak freely is unimpaired.[21]

The following case will emphasize the power possessed by the board to limit "freedom of speech." A teacher, also president of the teacher's union, was unsuccessful in his attempt to remove a reprimand by the board of education president from his file. The teacher complained about certain acts of a school principal to the board and was advised by the board to refrain from further comment until the board had completed its investigation. The teacher gave the news media his information contrary to board direction, and the resulting reprimand in his file was not deemed a violation of his liberty interests or equal protection under the law.[22]

---

[19]Schimmel, David and Louis Fischer: "On the Cutting Edge of the Law: The Expansion of Teacher's Rights." *The School Review*, p. 266, February 1974.

[20]McAuliff v. Mayor of New Bedford, Mass., 220, 29 N.E., 517 (1892).

[21]Van Alstyne: "The Demise of the Right-Privilege Distinction in Constitutional Law." *Harvard Law Review*, 81, 1439 (1968).

[22]Swilley v. Alexander, 448 F. Supp. 702 (S.D. Ala., 1978).

First Amendment rights will not protect a teacher who insists on discussing controversial matters in the classroom or the private sector, nor will these rights provide protection to a teacher who fails to make a balanced presentation of the prescribed subject matter. As stated by the New York State Commissioner of Education:

> ... subject matter involving conflicting opinions, theories or schools of thought, the teacher must present a fair summary of the entire range of opinions so that the student may have complete access to all facets and phases of the subject.[23]

Failure to make a balanced presentation has been viewed as evidence of a teacher's lack of fitness. It may reflect incompetence in the subject matter or an attempt to proselytize in the classroom.

Purposes of Academic Freedom

Academic freedom thus not only protects teachers from undue infringement of their constitutional rights while in the classroom, but it also provides them with a barrier against arbitrary actions by requiring the state to forewarn them, in clear and precise terms, of proscribed conduct. The requirement of adequate notice and clear, precise regulations is dictated by the due process clause of the Fourteenth Amendment.[24]

The First Amendment right to free speech may be viewed as having two main purposes: The first is affording each person a maximum right to accomplish his own goals for his life, and requiring that each person have the right to communicate freely with others. The second purpose is the protection of public interest by maximizing the flow of information to the people.[25]

Rights of Teachers Under Tenure

The tenure rights of teachers are generally statutorily defined. It is well established that states have the authority to pass tenure laws as part of their plenary power over education.[26] School

---

[23]Charles Jones, No. 8195, N.Y. State Education Department (September 23, 1970).

[24]Keefe v. Geanakos, 418 F.2d 359, 362 (1st Cir. 1969).

[25]Boote, Karen S.: "The Public School Teacher's Right to Criticize the School Administration." *NOLPE School Law Journal*, Vol. 5, No. 2, p. 141, 1975.

[26]State ex. rel. Glover J. Holbrook, 129 Fla. 241, 176 So. 99 (1937).

districts generally carry a heavy burden of proof when attempting to dismiss or discipline a tenured teacher because tenure rights are established to improve the educative enterprise by providing teachers adequate procedural safeguards before dismissal. A teacher cannot be dismissed for activities other than those specifically prohibited by tenure statutes or those deemed reasonable by the courts in light of legislative policy (*see* Chapter 2).

In addition to protecting teachers from arbitrary dismissals, tenure rights also shield teachers from other irresponsible actions by school authorities. For example, after acquiring tenure a teacher is guaranteed continued employment until resignation or retirement, subject only to the requirements of good behavior and financial necessity. In addition, tenure assures the teacher academic freedom in the exercise of First Amendment rights in the classroom subject only to regulations evidencing a compelling state interest; tenure assures protection from irresponsible actions by school officials. Other rights are enjoyed by tenured teachers:

1. A school board may not demote or reduce the salary of a tenured teacher without notice and a hearing.
2. A board may not reassign a teacher from one position or one school to another unless the new assignment is equal in professional status to the prior position.[27]
3. The right not to be dismissed or refused renewal of contract except for cause.
4. The right to certain dismissal protections:
   a. a written statement of reasons of the board's intention to terminate a contract;
   b. ten days to file a written request for a hearing, which may be public or private;
   c. if a hearing is requested, it must be scheduled within thirty days;
   d. the clerk must give written notice within fifteen days;
   e. a majority of the board must conduct the hearing;
   f. the board must provide a record of the hearing to the teacher;
   g. both parties must be represented by counsel;

---

[27]State v. Jefferson Parish School Board. 188 So. 2d 143 (la. Ct. App. 1966).

h. witnesses may be required to testify, within limitations;
i. the board by a majority of vote may terminate the contract;
j. if the teacher is rehired, the record is erased and back pay is given;
k. if the teacher is terminated, he may appeal to the court of common pleas within thirty days after notice of termination.

Abrogation of Tenure

Tenure privileges may be withdrawn because of fraudulent representation, retirement, death, voluntary resignation, repeal of statutory enactments granting tenure, and for cause through formal dismissal proceedings. The right of a legislative body to repeal tenure laws is dependent upon the form of the tenure. Contractual tenure cannot be repealed.

Dress and Appearance

The courts have recognized teacher's grooming to be protected as a form of symbolic speech under the First Amendment. The courts have granted this protection to teachers who against the wishes of the school authorities have worn beards, moustaches, goatees, and certain hair styles while teaching in the public schools. Even though teachers have won these rights in courts, many school boards believe that it is their responsibility to assure that a teacher's appearance is in accord with the professional standards of the community.

For example, the Tennessee Supreme Court held that a rule forbidding teachers to wear beards was reasonably related to the management of schools and did not violate a teacher's constitutional rights.[28] In a Louisiana case,[29] the courts upheld a school board regulation requiring men teachers to wear a necktie. The teacher claimed that the regulation was unrelated to any educational aim as well as being unreasonable infringement upon his liberty of dress. The court, however, went along with the

---

[28]Morrison v. Hamilton County Board of Education, 494 S.W.2d 770 (1973).
[29]Blanchet v. Vermillion School Board (La.) 220 S.2d 534 (1969).

contention of the Board that "wearing neckties enhanced the image of the teacher as a professional man, leading to more community and student respect for him."

In other cases, the supreme courts upheld the decisions rendered by previous courts. In Ramsey,[30] a federal district court characterized a rule against the wearing of moustaches by teachers as:

> . . . a gross example of a rule based upon personal taste of an administrative official which is not a permissible base upon which to build rules for the organization of a public institution. Here there is not the slightest of argument or evidence offered to support the proscription against moustaches . . . no evidence that moustaches had caused, or were likely to cause any disturbance; no evidence of any health or sanitation problem; no indication of difficulties of any sort with moustaches.

In another case, a federal district court struck down a high school grooming regulation that limited the length of an adult teacher's hair because it was irrelevant to any state interest and created "an arbitrary and capricious classification, devoid of logic and rationality"[31] that plainly offends both substantive due process and equal protection guaranteed by the Fourteenth Amendment.

In a 1967 case,[32] the court upheld the constitutional rights of teachers. Paul Finot taught government to high school seniors in the Pasadena, California school system. When he arrived at school wearing a beard, the high school principal asked him to shave it off. Upon his refusal, the Pasadena Board of Education transferred him to home teaching despite the fact that he was an excellent teacher. Finot sued to have the Board's decision overturned.

The board claimed the transfer was justified on the basis of the school's administrative policy as well as the professional judgment of the principal and superintendent. The administrative policy was based on the city's teacher handbook, which called for teachers to conform to acceptable dress and grooming, and to set an example of neatness and good taste.

---

[30]Ramsey v. Hopkins, 320 F. Supp. 477 (N.D. Ala., 1970).
[31]Conard v. Goolsby, 350 F. Supp. 713 (N.D. Miss., 1972).
[32]Finot v. Pasadena City Board of Education, 58 Cal. Rptr. 520 (1967).

The board further stated that the appearance of teachers had a definite effect on student's dress and conduct, that well-dressed students generally behaved well. The board felt Finot's beard might attract undue attention, interfere with the process of education, and make the prohibition against student beards more difficult to enforce. They believed that wearing a beard did not meet the school's requirement of acceptable grooming or set an example of good taste. A California court ruled against the school.

The court said that Finot's right to wear a beard was one of the liberties protected by the Fourteenth Amendment that prohibits the deprivation of life, "liberties," or property of any person without due process of law. Furthermore, the judge said that the "wearing of a beard is a form of expression of an individual's personality" and that such a right of expression is entitled to the "peripheral protection" of the First Amendment.[33]

The law concerning teacher's personal appearance is not universal. The U.S. Supreme Court has not ruled on the question, and the judges are divided on the issue. However, school boards are liberalizing both their dress and grooming codes, and "future courts may extend constitutional protection to all aspects of personal appearance."[34]

Freedom of Association

Generally, a public school teacher possesses certain freedoms enjoyed by all citizens. As a citizen, s/he has the right to speak, think, and believe as s/he wishes, subject to limitation of the Constitution. For example, the First Amendment places limitation by adding "peaceably." S/he may, with rare exceptions, affiliate with groups of his/her choice. As a public school teacher, however, s/he must exercise these and other legal rights with restricted discretion, and with due consideration of the effects upon others, particularly school children. Because of the position, "a government employee," s/he must conform to certain laws, rules, and regulations not equally applicable to citizens outside the teaching profession.

---

[33]*Supra* note 19, p. 272.
[34]*Supra* note 19, p. 273.

The right of association for teachers is a right guaranteed by the Constitution of the United States. However, this right is not an implicit proviso in the national or state constitution; this right is implied in the First Amendment. Like all other constitutional rights, the right of association does not exist without limitation. Because of the nature of the teaching profession, where the classroom teacher is expected to be a role model responsible for shaping young minds, the state may impose more limitations on his association than persons in other professions.

In one case, a teachers was dismissed for living with a male who was not her husband.[35] The teacher claimed that the dismissal was in violation of her constitutional rights to privacy and freedom of association. The federal district court held, however, that the state is entitled to protect the integrity of its schools, even if the plaintiff's conduct were constitutionally protected. The court found that the board could reasonably believe that the plaintiff's conduct could have a detrimental effect on her relations with her pupils, particularly in light of the adverse community action. The citizens had signed a petition against the teacher's conduct.

In another case, a male high school counselor spent the night with a recently graduated female student at her home. Her parents were away for the night. The board of education took action to dismiss the teacher on two charges. First, the board cited sexual misconduct, and second, the board charged that the teacher had repeatedly lied to school officials about the event, denying that he had in fact spent the night with the girl. The trial court found against the board on the first count stating:

> The private association of a teacher with a member of the opposite sex, is not by itself the concern of the defendant, except on a showing not here made that it may interfere with his responsibilities to his students and his ability to teach.[36]

The court found, however, that the second charge provided a basis for discipline and authorized the board to continue with a hearing on the administrative charge. Upon appeal, the appellate division held that the student-teacher sexual relationship was not

---

[35]Sullivan v. Meade City Independent School District, 387 F. Supp. 1237 (D.S.D., 1975).
[36]Goldin v. Board of Education, 45 App. Div. 2d 870, 357 N.Y.S.2d 867 (Sup. Ct., 1974).

a purely private behavior and sustained the board's action to dismiss.[37]

Another case involving freedom of association claims arose in the context of union membership activities. Three nontenured teachers whose contracts were not renewed brought suit alleging that they were terminated in violation of their First Amendment rights for their activities as members of a teacher's organization. The court held that if there was any evidence to support the reasons given by the board for nonrenewal, the board's actions would be upheld. The court refused to examine the validity of the reasons given by the board, declaring that since nontenured teachers are not entitled to a hearing before the school board to determine if there is any basis in fact for the decision, the federal courts may not conduct a hearing to make such a determination. The court then noted that the plaintiffs were unable to show that there was a "direct causal link" between the nonrenewal of the contracts and their union activities.[38]

Rights Outside the Classroom

There are no statutes that stipulate specifically what a teacher may or may not do outside of school hours and away from the school grounds. There are, however, statutes that authorize boards of education to dismiss teachers for conduct that becomes public through the indiscretion of the teacher. If the outside activity is of such a nature as to give a bad reputation to the teacher—reflect adversely on the profession—a school board would be within its rights in dismissing the teacher on the grounds "no longer effective," "conduct unbecoming a teacher," or "for other good and just cause." An increasing number of courts are holding that a teacher's private acts are his own business and should not form a basis for disciplinary action as long as his teaching competence is not affected.

Teachers' Strikes

"A teachers' strike is the cessation of work by a body of teachers

---

[37]Goldin v. Board of Education, 78 Misc. 2d 972, 359 N.Y.S.2d 384 (Sup. Ct., 1975).

[38]Phillippe v. Clinton-Prairie School Corp., 394 F. Supp. 316 (S.D. Ind., 1975).

for the purpose of forcing from the school board certain concessions pertaining to working conditions, salaries or other aspects of teacher welfare."[39]

The law governing the right of teachers to strike is still in the process of development. In 1951, a case dealing with this issue came before the Supreme Court of Errors of Connecticut. In an action for a declaratory judgment, certain questions were addressed to the court. One of these was: "May the plaintiff [the Norwalk Teachers' Association] engage in concerted action such as strike, work stoppage"? The court answered this question in the negative, saying in part:

> Under our system, the government is established by and run for all of the people, not for the benefit of any group or person. The profit motive inherent in the principle of free enterprise, is absent. It should be the aim of every employee of the government to do his or her part to make it function as efficiently and economically as possible. The drastic remedy of the organized strike to enforce demands of unions of government employees is in direct contravention of this principle.[40]

In most of the court cases reported, in which the legality of teachers' strike has been the issue, the courts have ruled that the teacher strike is illegal. Teachers who strike have been penalized in various ways: termination, fines, injunctions, and no pay increases being most common.

Termination

In Michigan, the Public Employment Relations Act prohibits strikes by teachers. The teachers of Lake Michigan Community College went out on strike in February, 1973. The board notified all striking teachers that their action was illegal and that if they did not return to work by a specific date, their employment would be terminated under the terms of the statute. Certain teachers failed to return to work on the specific date and were given notice of termination, including a notice that they were

---

[39]Bolmeier, Edward C.: *The School in the Legal Structure*. Cincinnati, Ohio: The W.H. Anderson Co., 1974, p. 219.

[40]Norwalk Teachers' Association v. Board of Education of City of Norwalk, 138 Conn. 269, 83 Atl. 2d 482.

entitled to a hearing. The federal district court ruled that the termination procedures under the Public Employment Relations Act did not provide the teachers with due process and granted relief against the college. The college appealed to the Court of Appeals for the Sixth Circuit. The circuit court reversed the district court, holding that the striking teachers did not enjoy the protection of the due process clause.[41]

Restraining Order

In an Indiana case, a superior court adjudged a teachers' union in contempt of court for violating a restraining order directing the union and its members to refrain from picketing and striking against the school.

On appeal, the order of the lower court was affirmed by the Supreme Court of Indiana. The court found that "the overwhelming weight of authority in the United States is that government employees may not engage in a strike for any purpose." In support of the lower court's ruling, the Supreme Court stated, in part: ". . . to allow a strike by public employees is not merely a matter of choice of political philosophies, but is a thing which cannot and must not be permitted if the orderly function of our society is to be preserved."[42]

Fines

In a New Jersey case, a teacher was convicted and fined 500 dollars for contempt of court for ignoring a temporary restraining order prohibiting striking. The strike was called against the Newark school system and the defendent teacher, along with some 1,700 others, did not report to work.[43]

Teachers in New York are subject to provisions of the so-called Taylor Law for public employees, which specifies two days pay deduction for each day missed because of an illegal strike.

---

[41]Lake Michigan College Federation of Teachers v. Lake Michigan Community College, 518 F. Supp. 1091 (W.D. Michigan, 1975).

[42]Anderson Federation of Teachers v. Schools, City of Anderson, 251 N.E.2d 18 (Indiana, 1969).

[43]New Jersey v. Brown, 50 N.J. 435, 236 A.2d 142 (1967).

Striking teachers have often challenged the constitutionality of
the law's provision for the salary deduction. In *Lawson v. Board
of Education of Vestal*, the members of a teachers' association
charged that the Taylor Law violated due process of law because
of the manner in which the violation is determined.[44] In *Zeluck v.
Board of Education of New Rochelle*, the challenge was based on
the denial of equal protection of the law because the provision
distinguishes between private and public employees and the
penalty constitutes a bill of attainder.[45]

Another method used to penalize striking teachers is legislation
prohibiting salary increases. Minnesota enacted a "no strike" law
requiring striking employees be terminated and that if s/he is
reemployed, no salary increase be given for a period of one year.

In a negotiated settlement following a strike, a board of
education agreed to reemploy teachers who had been on strike
and to pay them for the period of the strike.[46] The district court
enjoined the payment of these wages as a violation of the statute.
The teachers appealed, charging the statute violated their rights
under the First and Fourteenth Amendments.

The Minnesota Supreme Court rejected this claim stating:

> Public employees have no common law right to strike. It is
> clearly established common law that a strike by public employ-
> ees for any purpose is illegal. . . . An Indiana court earlier ruled
> that public employees do not have the right to strike and can
> only acquire it through legislation.[47]

From the forementioned cases, the courts have ruled that strikes
and other types of work stoppage are illegal. It is generally agreed
that it would be better for school boards and school personnel to
bargain (negotiate) in good faith, rather than use coercive tactics
or other illegal threats that could injure the school system and
cause damage to the community.

Summary

A public school teacher possesses certain rights and freedoms

---

[44]Lawson v. Board of Education of Vestal, 35 A.D.2d 878, 315 N.Y.S.2d 877 (1970).

[45]Zeluck v. Board of Education of New Rochelle, 62 Misc. 2d 274, 307 N.Y.S.2d 329 (Sup.
Ct., 1970).

[46]Head v. Special School District No. 1, 182 N.W.2d 887 (Minn., 1970); *also see* Topeka,
Kansas: NOLPE Mono. Series No. 2, 1972.

[47]Head v. Special School District No. 1, 182 N.W.2d 894 (Minn., 1970).

enjoyed by all citizens. As a citizen s/he has the legal right to speak, think, and believe as s/he wishes. As a public employee, however, s/he must exercise these and other legal rights with due consideration of the effect upon others, particularly school children.

It is difficult to delineate precisely the rights from the restraints. In trying to derive broad principles that would speak to the line of demarcation between rights and responsibilities, it must be borne in mind that virtually all rights afforded teachers have limitations. Even rights stipulated in the statutes and constitutions are not absolute as they pertain to teachers. Some of the Rights and Responsibilities follow:

1. As a teacher you enjoy freedom of speech and assembly, but this may be restricted by your position as an example for your students. Any support of unlawful conduct is clearly subject to restriction.
2. Although your mode of dress need not follow student standards, reasonable and nondiscriminatory rules must generally be followed.
3. Your freedom to teach and your selection of subject matter must reasonably relate to the age and maturity level of your students.
4. Employment cannot be conditioned on any political or religious belief or limited by membership in most organizations, nor can a teacher be required to salute the flag.
5. Your responsibility as a teacher carries over into your private life. The commodity you deal in is human minds. The standard to which you are held is high, but should not be arbitrary, capricious, or unrelated to sound educational objectives.

Compendium of Cases

FREEDOM OF ASSOCIATION. Three public school teachers in Mississippi were not rehired because they sent their children to a racially discriminatory private school.[48] The school board, which was under a school desegregation order, argued that the teachers would be less effective because their students would feel a sense of inferiority resulting from the teachers' rejection of their school

---

[48]Cook v. Hudson, 511 F.2d 744 (5th Cir., 1975).

for their own children.

The Fifth Circuit, in affirming the district court's decision upholding the board's action in the face of the teachers' claim that it violated their right of association, held that the action was within the discretion of the school board in deciding how to implement the desegregation order.

ACADEMIC FREEDOM. In Ahern v. Board of Education,[49] Frances Ahern sharply criticized another teacher for slapping a student. The criticism was voiced by Ms. Ahern to her high school economics class. Ahern then embarked on an extensive lesson on students' rights, during which the slapping incident was re-enacted and discussed. The administration learned of the lesson and Ms. Ahern was warned that the discipline of other teachers was the job of the administration. Ms. Ahern, however, continued with her students' rights discussions and was eventually dismissed for insubordination.

The court was persuaded that the school administration had an overriding interest in controlling what was said about another teacher in Ms. Ahern's classroom and in controlling what she taught and her dismissal was sustained.

FREEDOM OF EXPRESSION. In Florida, a federal district court held that the school board's failure to reappoint the only black teacher on the school faculty because he disobeyed an order to shave his goatee was arbitrary, discriminatory, and racially motivated. Therefore, the order of the board was nullified.[50]

In another case, the Tennessee Supreme Court held that a rule forbidding teachers to wear beards was reasonably related to the management of schools and did not violate a teacher's constitutional rights.[51]

STRIKES. According to a landmark decision of the United States Supreme Court, in 1976, the school boards have the constitutional right to fire illegally striking teachers with whom they are negotiating a work contract.[52] In North Dakota, three

---

[49]Ahern v. Board of Education, 327 F. Supp. 1391 (D. Neb., 1971).

[50]Braxton v. Board of Public Instruction of Duval County, 303 F. Supp. 477 (M.D. Fla., 1969).

[51]Morrison v. Hamilton County Board of Education, 494 S.W.2d 770 (1973).

[52]Hortonville Joint School District v. Hortonville Education Association, 96 S. Ct. 2308 (1976).

teachers were convicted of criminal contempt for violating an order enjoining picketing, work stoppages, or strikes.[53] The sheriff and his deputies testified they observed the three defendants walking back and forth carrying signs at the entrance to the Minot Air Force Base, the Minot High School, and the board of education, respectively. The teachers appealed, asserting, among other things, that the contempt statute was unconstitutional because it encroached on constitutional guarantees of freedom of speech and assembly, and because it permitted trial without a jury. These contentions were rejected by the state supreme court. The teachers were fined 250 dollars plus fifteen dollars court costs. Sentences of thirty days in jail were suspended on condition of good behavior, including no further picketing.

REFUSING NONCLASSROOM ASSIGNMENTS. In New York City, the Board of Education adopted the following policy:

1. Every teacher is required to give service outside of regular classroom instruction in the performance of functions which are essential duties of every teacher.
2. . . . The principal has the responsibility and duty to see that . . . activities are carried on. The principal may assign a teacher to reasonable amounts of such service beyond the specified hours of classroom instruction, and the teacher is required to render such service.
3. In the assignment of teachers to these activities, principals are directed to see to it that insofar as is practicable, such assignments are equitably distributed.[54]

The teachers sued, contending these resolutions unlawfully delegate to the individual principals of the schools the power to fix the duties and hours of the teachers without providing for adequate protection of the teachers.[55]

In disregarding the argument of the plaintiff teacher, the court upheld the validity of the board policy and at the same time, set forth the following guidelines:

Any teacher may be expected to take over a study hall; a teacher engaged in instruction in a given area may be expected

---

[53]North Dakota v. Heath, 177 N.W.2d 751 (N.D. 1970).
[54]Parrish v. Moss, 106 N.Y.S.2d 577 (1951).
[55]Parrish v. Moss, 106 N.Y.S.2d 581 (1951).

to devote part of his day to student meetings where supervision of such teacher is, in the opinion of the board, educationally desirable. Teachers in the fields of English and Social Studies and undoubtedly in other areas may be expected to coach plays; physical training teachers may be required to coach both intramural and interschool athletic teams; teachers may be assigned to supervise educational trips which are properly part of the school curriculum. . . . The board may not impose upon a teacher a duty foreign to the field of instruction for which he is licensed or employed. A board may not, for instance, require a mathematics teacher to coach intramural teams.[56]

CONDUCT DURING NONSCHOOL HOURS. In this case, the plaintiff teacher and her husband belonged to "The Swingers Club" devoted primarily to promoting diverse sexual activites between members of the party. Testimony revealed that:

... plaintiff has engaged in acts of sexual intercourse and oral copulation with men other than her husband; that . . . although plaintiff's services as a teacher have been "satisfactory," and although she is unlikely to repeat the sexual misconduct, nevertheless, she has engaged in immoral and unprofessional conduct.[57]

The board dismissed the teacher. The Supreme Court of California agreed with the board's action, and stated:

A teacher in the public school system is regarded by the public and pupils in the light of an exemplar, whose words and actions are likely to be followed by the children coming under her care and protection. . . . the Court concluded . . . that Mrs. Pettit's illicit and indiscreet actions disclosed her unfitness to teach in public elementary schools.[58]

---

[56]Parrish v. Moss, 106 N.Y.S.2d 584-585 (1951).
[57]Pettit v. State Board of Education, 10 Cal. App. 3d 29, 109 Cal. Rptr. 665 (1973).
[58]Pettit v. State Board of Education, 10 Cal. App. 3d 29, 109 Cal. Rptr. 667 (1973).

Chapter 7

CIVIL RIGHTS FOR THE HANDICAPPED

Introduction

A major legal development in the 1970s has been the extension of the principle of equal educational opportunities to all children, mainly the handicapped.

The most significant measure of the impact of this movement is the philosophy that handicapped persons should live and be treated like nonhandicapped persons to the greatest degree possible and that their differences from normal people can be reduced by minimizing the degree and circumstances to which they are treated differently from normal persons. "One step in minimizing differences is to recognize the claim that the handicapped have a right to education and that this right is equal to a normal person's right. An extension of this argument is the assertion that the educational opportunities granted to the normal pupil are constitutionally required to be granted to the handicapped."[1]

Until very recently equality of educational opportunities was no more than a distant, visionary goal. For some Americans, especially the handicapped, it has still not been attained. This is a point that professional educators and others stress about the rights of all Americans to equal educational opportunities, and it is basis for their charge that "limitations upon the civil liberties of the handicapped violate their constitutional rights to equal

[1]Turnbull,H. Rutherford. III: "Legal Aspects of Educating the Developmentally Disabled." In *Contemporary Legal Problems in Education*. Topeka, Kansas: NOLPE, 1975, pp. 174-175.

protection under the Fourteenth Amendment because there is no rational reason for imposing special burdens or limitations upon them that are not imposed upon normal persons."[2]

Historical Perspective

Prior to the 1960s, handicapped children were often excluded from the public schools or placed in substandard educational settings without any hearing regarding placement. The legality of denying a public education to handicapped children by exclusion or any other means is increasingly being challenged. The basis for this challenge can be found in the equal protection clause of the Fourteenth Amendment to the U. S. Constitution, which guarantees to all the people equal protection of the laws. The rights of the handicapped child to an education has been established in the courts. Two decisions stand out among many.

The Pennsylvania Association for Retarded Citizens brought an action against the Commonwealth of Pennsylvania in January, 1971, for the state's failure to provide access to a free public education for all retarded children. The defendants included the state secretaries of education and public welfare, the State Board of Education, and thirteen named school districts, representing the class of all Pennsylvania's school districts. The suit was resolved by a consent decree (decree entered by consent of all parties and the court) resting on the following findings:

1. The state could not apply any law which would postpone, terminate, or deny mentally retarded children access to a publicly supported education, including a public school program, tuition or tuition maintenance, and homebound instruction.
2. Local districts providing preschool education to any children were required to provide the same for mentally retarded children.
3. Local districts (state) were required to locate and identify all school-aged persons excluded from public schools; to provide thorough medical and physical evaluations of excluded children, children in special education programs, and children who were to be placed in those programs.

---

[2]*Supra* note 1.

4. Local districts were required to reevaluate each child in a special education program every two years or whenever a change in his program was planned.
5. The state and local districts were required to place all retarded children in a free public program of education and training appropriate to the child's capacity, with a preference for regular classes rather than special education.
6. By October 1971, the plaintiff children were to have been reevaluated and placed in programs, and by September 1972, all retarded children between the ages of six and twenty-one were to be provided a publicly supported education.[3]

In another case,[4] the parents and guardians of seven District of Columbia children brought a class action suit against the D. C. Board of Education, the Department of Human Resources, and the mayor for failure to provide all children with a publicly supported education.

The plaintiff children ranged in age from seven to sixteen and were alleged by the public schools to present the following types of problems leading to the denial of their opportunity for an education: slight brain damage, hyperactive behavior, epilepsy and mental retardation, and mental retardation with an orthopedic handicap.

The court ordered that (1) no child eligible for a publicly supported education be excluded from a regular school assignment because of any school rule, practice, or policy unless he is first provided with adequate alternative educational services suited to his needs, including special education or tuition grants and (2) with a constitutionally adequate prior hearing, periodic review of his status and progress, and periodic examination of the adequacy of any educational alternatives; (3) each child of school age must be provided suitable publicly supported education, regardless of the degree of the child's mental, physical, or emotional disability or impairment, without charge; (4) suitable education must be provided within thirty days to all handicapped children then known to the school authorities, and within fifty

---

[3]Pennsylvania Association for Retarded Children v. Commonwealth of Pennsylvania, 334 F. Supp. 1257 (E.D., 1971)

[4]Mills v. Board of Education of the District of Columbia, 348 F. Supp. 866 (D.D.C., 1972).

days to handicapped children who later came to the attention of the schools; (5) the availability of free public education for handicapped children must be advertised to identify previously excluded children and the reasons for their exclusions; (6) previously excluded children must be notified of the reasons for their exclusion and of their rights under the court order, and the educational needs of identified exceptional children must be evaluated; and (7) a proposal for placing each child in a suitable educational program must be filed with the court, to include the provision of compensatory educational services where required; a plan for identifying, notifying, evaluating, and placing the handicapped children; and a report showing eradication from or the correction of all official records of any of the plaintiffs in regard to past expulsions, suspensions, or exclusions affected by the violation of the due process requirements contained in the court order.

In both cases, the courts agreed with the contention of the plaintiffs. The Pennsylvania finding in favor of the retarded children was reinforced and expanded by the decision of the District of Columbia court ruling, which ordered schools to begin providing an equal education to all handicapped children. Similar suits began to turn up in other states, with consistent holdings supporting the rights of the handicapped. State legislatures got into the act following the court cases and enacted new laws to fund the education of handicapped children. In 1975, Congress passed P.L. 94-142.

P.L. 94-142—What It Is

Public Law 94-142 is the historic culmination of laws and litigation whose goal is to guarantee equal educational opportunities for all handicapped children. The law stipulates that in order for a state to receive federal funds for the education of handicapped children it must develop a comprehensive plan that ensures the provision of a free and appropriate education for all handicapped children.

More than any other legislation enacted to date, P.L. 94-142, the Education For All Handicapped Children Act, spells out the federal government's commitment to the education of all handicapped boys and girls with a plan to ensure the rights of these youngsters to a free and appropriate public education. The Education For All Handicapped Children Act calls for an expansion of the basic state grants program to provide a free, appropriate public education for all handicapped children between the ages of three and eighteen within the states by September 1978 and between the ages of three and twenty-one by 1980. In accomplishing these objectives, the state's first priority is to serve children currently unserved.

Other specific stipulations of P.L. 94-142 require:

1. State and local agencies to adopt policies that ensure all handicapped children the right to a free and appropriate public education.
2. Individual planning for the education of all handicapped children. This means that conferences among parents, children, and teachers must be held at least once a year.
3. Local educational agencies to provide, to the maximum extent appropriate, that handicapped children be educated with children who are not handicapped.
4. Proof by 1980 that free and appropriate public education is available to all handicapped children (3-21).
5. The development of a comprehensive system of personnel training, including preservice and in-service training for teachers.
6. Expansion of procedural safeguards "due process" for parents and children, securing their rights under the law.

Due Process and Least Restrictive Alternatives

Due process and least restrictive requirements, as they relate specifically to the public schools, were established by the decrees that evolved from both the Pennsylvania case[5] and the District of Columbia case[6]. In the former case, the court ruled that all

---

[5]Pennsylvania Association for Retarded Children v. Commonwealth of Pennsylvania, 334 F. Supp. 1257 (E.D., 1971).

[6]Mills v. Board of Education of the District of Columbia, 348 F. Supp. 866 (D.D.C., 1972).

mentally retarded children of school age were entitled to a free and appropriate education. Using the doctrine of the least restrictive alternative as applied to education, the court stated that, among alternative educational programs available, placement in a special public school class is preferable to placement in any other type of program of education and training.[7] The Pennsylvania decree was limited to the mentally retarded; in Mills, the court ordered implementation of equal educational opportunities for all handicapped children.

Least Restrictive Environment

P.L. 142 utilized two different terminologies that may be confusing to educators: least restrictive alternatives and least restrictive environment. The terminology is the same but allows for different interpretation.

Section 612 (5) (B) of the Act requires states to establish procedures to insure that (1) to the maximum extent appropriate, handicapped children are educated with children who are not handicapped and (2) removal of handicapped children from the regular educational environment occurs only when the nature or severity of the handicap is such that education in regular classes with the use of supplementary aids and services cannot be achieved satisfactorily.

These regulations (1) require each state educational agency about the least restrictive alternative provision, to assist them with its implementation, and to monitor their progress, (2) set forth all requirements designed to insure effective implementation of this provision for each handicapped child. In general, each public agency shall insure:

1. That to the maximum extent appropriate, handicapped children, including children in public or private institutions or other care facilities, are educated with children who are not handicapped, and

2. That special classes, separate schooling, or other removal of handicapped children from the regular educational environment occurs only when the nature or severity of the

[7]Aberson, A.: "Legal Forces and Pressures." In R.L. Jones (Ed.): *Mainstreaming the Minority Child.* Minneapolis, Minn.: The Council for Exceptional Children, 1976.

handicap is such that education in regular classes with the use of supplementary aids and services cannot be achieved satisfactorily.

Continuum of Alternative Placements

When it is clear that, because of the nature or severity of a child's handicap, the child must be educated in a setting other than the regular class, it is appropriate to implement such a placement. In respect to determining proper placements, each handicapped child's educational placement:

1. Is determined at least annually.
2. Is based on his or her individualized program.
3. Is as close as possible to the child's home.
4. Is, unless the handicapped child's individualized education program requires some other arrangement, in the school that he or she would attend if not handicapped.
5. Must, in selecting the least restrictive environment, consider any potential harmful effects on the child or the quality of services that he or she needs.

The parents' right to challenge the placement of their child extends not only to placement in special classes or separate schools but also to placement in a distant school, particularly in a residential program.

Due Process Procedures for Parents and Children

Sections 121 a. 500 through 121 a. 514 of Subpart E (P.L. 94-142) set forth requirements to ensure that handicapped children and their parents are guaranteed procedural safeguards with respect to requirements that such children be provided with a free and appropriate public education.

After locating the handicapped children, school authorities are required to evaluate them and place them in appropriate programs. However, prior to placement, it is required that the child's parents or guardian be notified in writing by registered mail. The notification must include all information relevant to the activity for which consent is sought, in his or her native language or other mode of communication. The parent must understand and agree in writing to the carrying out of the activity for which his or her consent is sought, and the consent must describe that activity and list the records (if any) that will be released and to whom; and the parent or guardian must understand that the granting of consent is voluntary on their part and can be repealed at any time. At a minimum, the notice should describe the proposed placement action and the reasons for it (including any tests or reports on which the action is based) and alternative educational opportunities available to the child, and must inform the parent or guardian that he has a right to object to the proposed action at a hearing and that medical, psychological, and educational evaluations are available free of charge.

If the parent or guardian requests a hearing, it is required to be conducted by a hearing officer independent of the local school authorities at a time and place convenient to the parent or guardian, between twenty and forty-five days after school authorities receive the request for a hearing (the twenty day minimum is waivable). It is to be closed unless the parent or guardian requests otherwise. The parent or guardian is to be informed that at the hearing he has a right to be represented by counsel, to present evidence and testimony, and to confront and cross-examine witnesses. In addition, he has a right to examine school records before the hearing and to be furnished with a transcript of the hearing if he wishes to appeal the decision of the hearing officer. A written statement that includes the decision, findings of fact, and conclusions of law is to be sent to the parent or guardian.

Independent Educational Evaluation

If a parent or guardian disagrees with a school district's evaluation of their handicapped child, they must be afforded the opportunity to obtain an independent evaluation. Basically, the school district must pay for such an evaluation if the parents disagree with the evaluation obtained or provided by the local educational agency. However, the local educational agency may initiate a hearing to show that its evaluation is appropriate. In such cases, if the final decision supports the school district's contention, then the parents or guardians are still entitled to an independent evaluation, but not at public expense. School districts are required to tell parents where they can obtain an independent evaluation, if they so request it.

Due Process Hearing

Due process requires that a hearing be held before a child can be placed in special education programs or transferred within them or excluded from them or excluded from school. In addition, local agencies must provide parents with information concerning free or low-cost legal and other relevant services that are available in connection with the hearing process. The statutes specify that a hearing may not be conducted by an employee of the agency from which the handicapped child receives an education or care. A person serving as a hearing officer may not have a personal or professional interest that would conflict with his or her objectivity in the hearings. This disqualifies parents from serving as hearing officers. A person meeting the conditions of impartiality, who is paid by an agency to serve as a hearing officer, would not be considered an employee of the agency. Each public agency must keep a list of persons who serve as hearing officers.

Any party to a hearing has the right to:

1. Be accompanied and advised by counsel and by individuals with special knowledge or training with respect to the problems of handicapped children.
2. Present evidence and confront, cross-examine, and compel the attendance of witness(es).
3. Prohibit the introduction of any evidence at the hearing that has not been disclosed to that party at least five days before the hearing.
4. Obtain a written or electronic verbatim record of the hearing.
5. Obtain written findings of fact and decisions.

Child's Status during Proceedings

A child's initial placement may not be changed during a complaint proceeding, unless the parents and agency agree otherwise. During the pendency of any administrative or judicial proceeding regarding a complaint, unless both parties agree otherwise, the child involved in the complaint must remain in his or her present educational placement. If the complaint involves an applicant for initial admission to public school, the child, with the consent of the parents, must be placed in the public school program until the completion of all the proceedings.

Protection in Evaluation Procedures

A concern for the procedures used in placing children within the school system is shown in the cases challenging the use of IQ tests, because of their linguistic and cultural bias, for purposes of determining intelligence and student tracking.[8]

The following two cases are cited as an example of misuse of placement using IQ testing.

In January, 1970, a suit was filed in the District Court of Northern California on behalf of nine Mexican-American students, ages 8 to 13.[9] The children came from homes in which Spanish was the major language spoken. The plaintiffs were assigned to mentally retarded classes in Monterrey County, California; their IQs ranged from 30 to 72. Upon being retested in Spanish, seven of the nine scored higher than the IQ cut-off for mental retardation, and the lowest score was only three points below the cut-off line.

The plaintiffs charged that the testing procedures utilized for placement were prejudicial, because the tests placed heavy emphasis on verbal skills requiring facility with the English language, the questions were culturally biased, and the tests were standardized on white, native-born Americans. The plaintiffs further pointed out that nearly one-third of the Spanish sur-named children in Monterrey County constituted the educable mentally retarded classes.

In 1966-67, studies by the California State Department of Education corroborated the inequity. The Department of Education found children with Spanish surnames comprised 26 percent of the educable mentally retarded population while they accounted for only 13 percent of the total school population.

---

[8]Guadalupe Organization v. Temple Elementary School District No. 3, Civ. No. 71-435 (D. Ariz., 1972).

[9]Diana v. State Board of Education, Civil No. C-70, 37 RFP (N.D. Cal., Jan. 1970).

The plaintiffs sought a class action suit on behalf of all bilingual Mexican-American children in classes for the educable mentally retarded. On February 5, 1970, a stipulated agreement order was signed by both parties. The order required that:

1. Children are to be tested in their primary language.
2. Mexican-American and Chinese children in classes for educable mentally retarded are to be retested and reevaluated.
3. Special efforts are to be extended to help misplaced children readjust to regular classrooms.

Another case[10] was filed as a class action in 1971 on behalf of six black, elementary-school-aged children. It was alleged that they had been inappropriately classified as educable mentally retarded and placed in classes for such children. The complaint argued that the children were not mentally retarded but rather victims of a testing procedure that failed to recognize their unfamiliarity with white, middle-class culture. The tests ignored the learning experiences the children may have had in their homes. The defendants included state and local school officials and board members.

On June 20, 1972, the court enjoined the San Francisco Unified School District from placing black students in classes for educable mentally retarded on the basis of IQ tests as currently administered, if the consequence of using such tests is racial imbalance in the composition of EMR classes.

Section 612 (5) (c) of P.L. 94-142 requires states to establish nondiscriminatory testing procedures for use in evaluation and placement of handicapped children. These requirements are designed to ensure that children are not misclassified or unnecessarily labeled as being handicapped because of inappropriate selection, administration, or interpretation of evaluation materials.

This act stipulates that state and local educational agencies shall ensure, at a minimum, that:

A. Tests and other evaluation materials:
   1. Are provided and administered in the child's native language or other mode of communication, unless it is clearly not feasible to do so;
   2. Have been validated for the specific purpose for which

---

[10]Larry P. v. Riles, Civil No. C-71-2270, 343 F. Supp. 1306 (N.D. Cal., 1972).

they are used; and

3. Are administered by trained personnel in conformance with the instructions provided by their producer.

B. Tests and other evaluation materials include those tailored to assess specific areas of educational need and not merely those which are designed to provide a single general intelligence quotient.

C. Tests are selected and administered so as best to ensure that when a test is administered to a child with impaired sensory, manual, or speaking skills, the test results accurately reflect the child's aptitude or achievement level or whatever other factors the test purports to measure, rather than reflecting the child's impaired sensory, manual, or speaking skills (except where those skills are the factors which the test purports to measure).

D. No single procedure is used as the sole criterion for determining an appropriate educational program for the child.

E. The evaluation is made by a multidisciplinary team or group of persons, including at least one teacher or other specialist with knowledge in the area of suspected disability.

F. The child is assessed in all areas related to the suspected disability, including, where appropriate, health, vision, hearing, social and emotional status, general intelligence, academic performance, communicative status, and motor abilities.

Parents Access to Records

The language of Section 121 a. 562 of P.L. 94-142 has been amended to make it clear that an agency must comply with a request for access to educational records before any meeting regarding an individualized education program can take place. In addition, each participating agency shall keep a record of parties obtaining access to education records collected, maintained, or used (except access by parents and authorized employees of the participating agency), including the name of the party, the date access was given, and the purpose for which the party was authorized to use the record.

If any education record includes information on more than one child, the parents of those children shall have the right to inspect and review only the information relating to their child or to be informed of that specific information.

FEES. A participating education agency may charge a fee for copies of records made for parents if the fee does not effectively prevent the parents from exercising their right to inspect and review those records. A participating agency may not charge a fee to search for or to retrieve information.

SUMMARY OF ACCESS RIGHTS

    A. Each participating agency shall permit parents to inspect and review any education records relating to their children that are collected, maintained, or used by the agency. The agency shall comply with a request without unnecessary delay and before any meeting regarding an individualized education program or hearing relating to the identification, evaluation, or placement of the child, and in no case more than forty-five days after the request has been made.

    B. The right to inspect and review education records, by parents, includes:

        1. The right to a response from the participating agency for reasonable requests for explanation and interpretation of the records;

        2. The right to request that the agency provide copies of the records containing the information if failure to provide those copies would effectively prevent the parent from exercising the right to inspect and review the records; and

        3. The right to have a representative of the parent inspect and review the records.

    C. Any agency may presume that the parent has authority to inspect and review records relating to his or her child unless the agency has been advised that the parent or guardian does not have the authority under applicable state law governing such matters as guardianship, separation, and divorce.

Amendment of Records

A parent who believes that information in education records collected, maintained, or used is inaccurate or misleading or violates the privacy or other rights of the child may request that participating agency which maintains the information to amend the information. The agency shall decide whether to amend the information in accordance with the request within a reasonable period of time of receipt of the request. If the agency decides to refuse to amend the information in accordance with the request, it shall inform the parent of the refusal, and advise the parent of the right to a hearing.

If, as a result of the hearing, the agency decides that the information is inaccurate, misleading, or otherwise in violation of the privacy or other rights of the child, it shall amend the information accordingly and so inform the parents in writing.

If, as a result of the hearing, the agency decides that the information is not inaccurate, misleading, or otherwise in violation of the privacy or other rights of the child, it shall inform the parents of the right to place in the records it maintains on the child a statement commenting on the information or setting forth any reason for disagreeing with the decision of the agency.

1. Any explanation placed in the records of the child must be maintained by the agency as part of the records of the child as long as the record or contested portion is maintained by the agency; and
2. If the records of the child or the contested portion is disclosed by the agency to any party, the explanation must also be disclosed to the party.

Summary

More than any other legislation enacted to date, P.L. 94-142, Education For All Handicapped Children Act, spells out the federal government's commitment to the education of all handicapped boys and girls with a plan to ensure the rights of these youngsters to a free and appropriate public education. The act holds that:

• Full educational services must be provided for handicapped children not currently receiving a free and appropriate public education;
• Full educational services must be provided for severely handicapped boys and girls receiving inadequate assistance;

- Parents or guardians have the right to examine all relevant records of the child as well as the right to obtain an independent educational evaluation of the child;
- Parents or guardians must be given written prior notice in their native language whenever the school proposes to initiate a change or refuse to initiate a change in regards to the identification, evaluation, or educational placement of the child;
- Parents or guardians have the right to present complaints with respect to the identification, evaluation, or educational placement of the child;
- Upon presentation of a complaint, the parents or guardians shall have an opportunity for an impartial hearing (in the hearing, they are to be given the right to be accompanied and advised by counsel);
- Parents or guardians shall be granted the right to a written or electronic verbatim record of such hearings and the right to written findings of fact and decisions;
- Any party aggrieved by the decision has the right to appeal to the state educational agency and ultimately the right to bring a civil action; and
- Whenever the parents or guardians of the child are not known, the state must assign an individual who is not an employee of the local or state educational agency to act as a surrogate for the parents.

Questions and Answers—P.L. 94-142

Q: What is the major purpose of P.L. 94-142?

A: The Education For All Handicapped Children Act (Public Law 94-142) was passed by Congress in November, 1975, in an effort to provide full educational opportunities for all handicapped children. Under its provisions, the law provides that in all states accepting federal funds, students are to receive a free and appropriate public education, regardless of handicap. In addition, these states are required to locate and serve all their handicapped children between the ages of three and eighteen by 1978, and between three and twenty-one by 1980. Utilizing the "right to education" doctrine, the court has ruled that school systems must provide all children equal opportunities to develop their own capabilities by providing different programs and facilities for pupils with different needs, according to their needs and abilities.

Q: What is the definition of a handicapped person under P.L. 94-142?

A: Handicapped children are those suffering any type impairment, such as those judged as being mentally retarded, hard of hearing, deaf, speech impaired, visually handicapped, seriously emotionally disturbed, orthopedically impaired, other health impaired, deaf-blind, multihandicapped, or as having specific learning disabilities, who because of those impairments need special education and related services.

Q: What is meant by "Special Education"?

A: Special education means specially designed instruction, at no cost to the parents* or guardians, to meet the unique needs of a handicapped child, including classroom instruction, instruction in physical education, home instruction, and instruction in hospitals and institutions. Special education includes speech pathology, audiology, occupational therapy, and physical therapy.

Q: What are related services?

A: Related services means transportation and such developmental, corrective, and other supportive services as are required to assist a handicapped child to benefit from special education, and includes speech pathology† and audiology, psychological services, physical and occupational therapy, recreation, early identification and assessment of disabilities in children, counseling services, and medical services for diagnostic or evaluation purposes. Related services are extended to include school social work services, parent counseling and training, providing parents with information about child development, and assisting parents in understanding the special needs of their child.

Q: What services must be provided under "physical education"?

A: Education in physical education includes the development of:

---

*"Parent" includes a parent, a guardian, a surrogate parent, or a person acting as a parent of a child in the absence of a parent or guardian.

†Some states include speech pathology, audiology, occupational therapy, and physical therapy under "special education," others under "related services."

- Physical and motor fitness;
- Fundamental motor skills and patterns;
- Skills in aquatic, dance, and individual and group games and sports (including intramural and lifetime sports);
- Special physical education, adapted physical education, and motor development.

Q: How is vocational education defined for handicapped students?

A: Vocational education is defined under the Vocational Education Act of 1963, as amended by P.L. 94-482, and includes industrial arts, consumer education, homemaking education programs as well as any organized educational programs directly related to the preparation of individuals for paid or unpaid employment, or for additional preparation for a career requiring other than a baccalaureate or advanced degree, at no expense to parents. However, incidental fees can be charged handicapped students for any programs normally charged to nonhandicapped students or their parents as part of the regular education program.

Q: On what basis can handicapped children be excluded from regular physical education programs?

A: The act (P.L. 94-142) states each handicapped child must be afforded the opportunity to participate in the regular physical education program available to nonhandicapped children unless:

- The child is enrolled full-time in a separate facility;
- The child needs specially designed physical education, as prescribed in the child's individualized education program;
- The child's participation is medically prohibited; or
- The parent objects to the child's inclusion in the program. The Fourteenth Amendment gives the parent the right to determine the subject matter his/her child can be required to take. However, they cannot mandate the method of instruction.

Each handicapped student receiving a free appropriate public education must be afforded physical education services, specially designed if necessary. If specially designed in a child's individual program, the agency responsible for the education of the child shall provide the services directly or make arrangements for it to be provided through the other public or private programs.

Q: What is meant by mainstreaming of the handicapped child?

A: The new law encourages that, to the maximum extent "appropriate," handicapped children, including children in public or private institutions or other care facilities, are educated with children who are not handicapped. The "maximum extent appropriate" will vary with each child. In some cases, the child will spend much of the day in a special class setting with only a brief time in a regular classroom. In other cases, a child may become completely integrated into a regular classroom. It depends on:

   a. the classes that are appropriate to the child's ability to adjust;
   b. the desires of the parents;
   c. the least restrictive environment; and
   d. the individual education program.

Q: Is individualized instruction required under the law?

A: It is a must. The statute requires that an individual education program (IEP) be established for each handicapped student enrolled in a free appropriate educational setting. The individualized educational program is a written statement developed in conjunction with the child's teacher, a representative of local school district, the parents, under certain circumstances a member of the evaluation team, and the child, when appropriate. There must be at least one conference a year to plan the child's education program, set goals, evaluate progress, and tailor educational activities to each child's particular needs. This means that valid assessments, behavioral objectives, sequential activities, and individual counseling must be a part of "individualization" and program planning for every handicapped child.

Each educational agency must provide assurance that it will establish, or revise, whichever is most appropriate, an individualized program for each handicapped child at the beginning of each school year and will review or revise the provisions of such programs, at least annually.

Q: Who determines the individual education program?

A: Generally, the composition of the team is:
- A representative of the local school district;
- The child's teacher;
- A special education teacher;
- One or both parents or guardians;
- The child when appropriate;
- Other individuals at the discretion of the parents or local school board.

The parents' participation and cooperation in establishing the child's program is essential. Their input and understanding is crucial if one is to avoid future litigation and utmost cooperation. The importance of parental involvement cannot be overstressed.

The act states that each agency shall take the necessary steps to ensure that one or both parents are present at each meeting or are afforded the opportunity to participate. The agency should notify the parents of the meeting in sufficient time to ensure they will have ample time to make preparations to attend. The meeting should be scheduled at a mutually agreed on time. (This mutual time should be at the parents' convenience.)

After exhausting all methods to involve the parents, if they refuse to attend, the agency, by law, can conduct the meeting without the parents in attendance. The act does not limit the ways an agency must attempt to contact parents for attendance at the meetings. The procedure used to notify the parents, whether oral or written, or both, is left to the discretion of the agency, but the agency must keep a record of its efforts. If the meeting is conducted without parental involvement, the minimum safeguards recommended are:

1. Records should be kept of the agency efforts to arrange mutually agreed upon time(s) and site(s);
2. Detailed records of telephone calls between agency and parents and the results of calls;
3. Copies of all correspondence and results; and
4. Records of visitation(s), attempted visitation(s) and results.

Q: What items must be contained in each Individualized Educational Program?

A: The essential items that must be contained in each IEP are:
1. A statement of the child's present levels of educational performances;
2. A statement of annual goals, including short term instructional objectives;
3. A statement of the specific special education and related services to be provided to the child, and the extent to which the child will be able to participate in regular educational programs; i.e., the amount of time each child will be mainstreamed;
4. Appropriate objective criteria and evaluation procedures and schedule for determining whether short term objectives are being achieved. However, the agency does not violate the required regulations if the child does not achieve the rate of growth projected in the annual stated goals and objectives.

Q: How is the initial placement of a handicapped child determined?

A: The overriding rule is that placement decisions must be made on an individual basis. This placement must be made after an analysis of a variety of sources, including aptitude and achievement tests, teacher recommendations, physical condition, social or cultural background, and adaptive behavior. There must be evidence that the information obtained from all of these sources is documented and carefully considered. In addition, there must be assurance that the placement decision is made by a group of persons, including persons knowledgeable about the child, the meaning of the evaluation data, and the placement options; there must be assurance that the placement decision is made in conformity with the least restrictive alternatives. With respect to determining proper placements, it is stressed that where a handicapped child is disruptive in a regular classroom, so that the education of other students is significantly impaired, the needs of the handicapped child cannot be met in that environment. Therefore, regular placement will not be appropriate to his/her needs. If students are to be placed in an alternate setting, among factors to be considered in placing a child is the need to place the child as close to home as possible. The parents' right to challenge the placement of their child extends not only to placement in special classes or separate schools, but also to placement in a distant school, particularly in a residential program.

Unless a handicapped child's individualized education program requires some other arrangement, the child is educated in the school he or she would attend if not handicapped; in selecting placement, consideration must be given to any potential harmful effect on the child or on the quality of services he or she needs. In placement, each local agency shall ensure:

1. That to the maximum extent appropriate, handicapped children, including children in public or private institutions or other care facilities, are educated with children who are not handicapped; and

2. That special classes, separate schooling, or other removal of handicapped children from the regular educational environment occurs only when the nature or severity of the handicap is such that education in regular classes with the use of supplementary aids and services cannot be satisfactorily achieved.

Q: What are the protections in evaluation procedures?

A: The act requires states to establish nondiscriminatory testing procedures for use in the evaluation and placement of handicapped children. These requirements are designed to ensure that children are not misclassified or unnecessarily labeled as being handicapped because of inappropriate selection, administration, or interpretation of evaluation materials. All testing and evaluation materials and procedures used for the purposes of evaluation and placement of handicapped children must be selected and administered so as not to be racially or culturally discriminatory. All materials are provided and administered in the child's native language or other mode of communication (if not in his or her native language, an interpreter must be present); evaluation materials must have been validated for the specific purpose for which they are used; evaluation materials are administered by trained personnel in conformance with the instructions provided by their producer; tests and other evaluation materials include those tailored to assess specific areas of educational need; tests are selected and administered so as best to ensure that, when a test is administered, the test results accurately reflect the child's aptitude or achievement level or whatever other factors the test purports to measure, rather than the extent of the child's disability; no single procedure is used as the sole criteria for placement; the evaluation is made by a multidisciplinary team or group of persons; and the child is assessed in all areas related to suspected disability. Children who have a speech impairment as their primary handicap may not need a complete battery of assessments (e.g., psychological, physical, or adaptive behavior). However, a qualified speech-language pathologist should evaluate the child using appropriate procedures for the diagnosis and appraisal of speech and language disorders.

Q: What are the rights of parents prior to placement and changes in the placement of their child?

A: Prior to placing a child in a program, the parents must give their consent. "Consent" means that:

1. The parent has been informed fully of all information relative to the purposes of testing, evaluation and all activities leading to the placement, in his or her native language, or other mode of communication
2. The parent understands and agrees in writing to this placement;
3. The parents understand that the granting of consent is voluntary and may be revoked at any time.

However, if there is disagreement as to the placement of the child based on the evaluations, the parents have the right to obtain an independent evaluation. This independent evaluation must be conducted by a qualified examiner who is not employed by the public agency responsible for the education of the child in question. In addition, the public agency must provide the parent, on request, information about where an independent educational evaluation may be obtained. The first independent evaluation must be at the public's expense. After the parent has been afforded an independent evaluation and has presented the evidence to the local agency, regardless of the findings, the local agency has the right to conduct a hearing. If the final decision is that the agency evaluation is appropriate, the parent has the right to disagree, and request another independent evaluation, but not at public expense.

If the parents obtain an independent educational evaluation at private expense, the result of the evaluation:

1. Must be considered by the public agency in any decision made with respect to the provisions of a free appropriate public education to the child; and

2. May be presented as evidence at a hearing regarding the placement of the child. If the hearing officer upholds the agency, the agency may:

   a. obtain a court order authorizing the agency to provide the education and related services; or

   b. may use due process procedures to obtain a decision to allow the evaluation or services without parental consent.

The agency must notify the parents of its actions, and the parents have appeal rights as well as rights at the hearing itself.

Q: What is the procedure for conducting the hearing?

A: A hearing may not be conducted by an employee of the agency from which the handicapped child receives an education or care. A person serving as a hearing officer may not have a personal or professional interest that would conflict with his or her objectivity in the hearings. A person meeting the conditions of impartiality, who is paid by an agency to serve as a hearing officer, would not be considered an employee of the agency. However, a parent of the child as well as school board officials are disqualified to conduct a hearing. Any party to a hearing has the right to:

- Be accompanied and advised by counsel and by individuals with special knowledge or training with respect to the problems of handicapped children;

- Present evidence and confront, cross-examine, and compel the attendance of witnesses;

- Prohibit the introduction of any evidence at the hearing

that has not been disclosed to the party at least five days before the hearing;

- Obtain a verbatim record of the hearing.

Parents must be given the right to have the child present and to open the hearing to the public.

Q: What rights do parents have to appeal a decision?

A: If the hearing is conducted by a public agency other than the state educational agency, any party aggrieved by the findings may appeal to the state educational agency. The state agency shall conduct an impartial review of the hearing. The official conducting the review shall:

- Examine the entire hearing record;
- Ensure that the procedures at the hearing were consistent with the requirements of due process;
- Afford the parties an opportunity for oral or written argument, or both, at the discretion of the reviewing official;
- Make an independent decision on completion of the review; and
- Give a copy of written findings and the decision to the parties.

The decision made by the reviewing official is final unless a party brings a civil action.

Q: What are the procedures during a civil action?

A: The public agency shall ensure that no longer than 45 days after the receipt of a request for a hearing:

1. A final decision is reached in the hearing; and
2. A copy of the decision is mailed to each of the parties.

The state educational agency shall ensure that not later than 30 days after the receipt of a request for a review:

1. A final decision is reached in the review; and
2. A copy of the decision is mailed to each of the parties;
3. A hearing or review officer may grant specific extensions of time beyond the periods set at the request of either party;
4. Each hearing and each review involving oral arguments must be conducted at a time and place which is convenient to the parents and child involved.

Q: Who is responsible for in-service training of teachers and others engaged in teaching handicapped students?

A: Sections 121 a. through 121 a. 387 implement the statutory requirement that a state develop and implement a comprehensive system of personnel development including in-service training* of general and special education instructional and support personnel. Section 121 a. 382 specifies that the state's educational agency annual program must:

1. Conduct an annual needs assessment to determine if a sufficient number of qualified personnel are available in the state;
2. Initiate in-service personnel development program based on the needs assessment; i.e.,
   a. New and additional personnel needs;
   b. Need for retraining personnel;
   c. State educational agency must ensure that ongoing in-service training programs are available to all personnel who are engaged in the education of handicapped children, and these programs include:
      (1) The use of incentives that ensure participation by teachers (such as released time, payment for participation, options for academic credit, salary step credit, certification renewal, or updating professional skills);
      (2) The involvement of local staff; and
      (3) The use of innovative practices.

For a fuller treatment of the questions and answers above see "Final Regulations for Public Law 94-142, Education For All Handicapped Children Act of 1975, *Federal Register*, Volume 42, No. 163. Also the Administrative Hearing under PL 94-142, *School Law in Contemporary Society*, NOLPE, pp. 265-270, 1980.

---

*"In-service training" means any training other than that received by an individual in a full-time program which leads to a degree.

HISTORICAL HIGHLIGHTS
OF CERTIFICATION

1806-21   There were no judgments made of teacher fitness.

1821-25   District committees were established to evaluate teachers.

1825   First certification law, in Ohio. Common Pleas court in each county appointed annually three examiners. A certificate from the county was required.

1831   State law named areas of qualification: reading, writing, and arithmetic.

1836   Township, not county, became the certification unit.

1838   Subject fields were listed on certificates, and the control was returned to the county.

1864   First state participation in certification. State Board of Examiners issued life certificates. The certificate was valid statewide.

1894   Uniform examination questions were issued by the state, but administered locally.

1914   The State Board of Education was authorized to grant four-year certificates throughout the state on the basis of academic professional training; two years for elementary certification; four years for high school certification, including supervised teaching.

1919   Vocational subjects and kindergarten were added to certificates.

1933   State Department of Education granted provisional certificates (statewide); state examiners granted life certificates (statewide); and local examiners granted county-wide certificates.

1935   Certification laws were revised. Local examiners and state examiners were removed. All certificates were granted by the State Department of Education, and issued according to a pattern of training prescribed by the Director of Education.

Principal and supervisory certificates were issued to holders of eight-year certificates on the recommendation of their superintendents.

Superintendent certificates were issued to holders of eight-year teaching certificates and the master's degree.

1939   Applicants for elementary certification must have completed three years of college training.

1948   Elementary cadet certificates were introduced due to teacher shortage.

1951   Applicants for elementary certification must have completed a degree program.

1955   Administrators were required to complete graduate work in areas of administration and supervision. The executive head certificate was initiated.

1964   The master's degree was required for all administrative certificates. The educational administrative specialist's certificate was initiated.

1966   The cadet certification was dropped; the last certificate was issued in 1968. All applicants for eight-year elementary certification must have completed the bachelor's degree plus 18 semester or 27 quarter hours of course work beyond the degree.

1972   The planned field experience was initiated for administrators.

1975   The school nurse certificate was initiated.

1977   Certification standards for teachers of the moderately, severely, and profoundly retarded were adopted by the State Board of Education. These standards took effect January 1, 1979.

GLOSSARY

Abatement—Termination of a lawsuit.

Appellant—Party who brings action in a higher court.

Appellee—Party against whom action is brought in a higher court.

Assault—A threat or attempt to inflict bodily injury where the victim has reason to believe the injury may be inflicted.

Battery—An unlawful beating or other wrongful physical violence inflicted on another.

Caveat emptor—Let the buyer beware.

Certiorari—Proceeding in which a higher court reviews a decision of an inferior court.

Class action—A law suit brought by one or more persons on behalf of all persons similarly situated as to complaint and remedy sought.

Code—A compilation of statutes, scientifically arranged.

Common law—Legal principles derived from usages and customs, as distinguished from law created by constitutions and statutes and court interpretations thereof.

Complaint—A plaintiff's first formal pleading in a civil suit. This document, filed with the court and delivered to the defendant, is intended to inform the defendant of the factual grounds upon which the plaintiff is relying in his lawsuit.

Criminal liability—Liability to fine or imprisonment or both, as distinguished from civil liability to compensate by paying damages.

De facto—In reality, actually.

De jure—By a lawful title, of right. By action of law.

Declatory Judgment—That form of judgment rendered by a court in which only a declaration of the rights of the parties or an opinion on a question of law is given. Unlike most judgments in civil actions, a declaratory judgment does not require or order anything to be done pursuant to the judgment rendered.

Defendant—Party against whom an action is brought.

Demurrer—Allegations to the effect that, even if facts asserted by plaintiff are true, these facts do not give rise to a legal cause of action.

Dictum—An opinion or observation expressed by a judge, in pronouncing his decision upon a cause, which is addressed to a point not necessarily arising or involved in the case in question or necessary for determining the rights of the involved parties.

Dissenting Opinion—The opinion in which a judge announces his dissent from the conclusions held by the majority of the court.

Due process—The exercise of the powers of government in such a way as to protect individual rights.

Enjoin—To require a person, by writ of injunction from a court of equity, to perform, or to abstain or desist from, some act.

Et al.—And others. When the words "et al." are used in an opinion, the court is thereby indicating that there are unnamed parties, either plaintiffs or defendants, also before the court in the case.

Estoppel—A bar raised by the law that prevents one from alleging or denying a certain fact because of his previous statements or conduct.

Ex Post Facto Law—A law passed after an occurrence, and which retrospectively changes the legal consequences of that act.

Ex rel. (Ex relatione)—An informational phrase: a legal proceeding instituted in the name and on behalf of the state but on information and at the instigation of an individual who has a private interest in the matter.

Injunction—A judicial order requiring the person or persons to whom it is addressed to do or not to do a particular act or acts.

In Loco Parentis—Replacing a parent; in the place of a parent, having some of the rights and duties of a parent.

Invalid—Not binding; lacking in authority.

Ipso Facto—By the facts itself.

Laches—Neglect to do something at the proper time; an undue delay to do a thing that should be done or failure to enforce a right at the time required.

Majority opinion—The statement of reasons for the views of the majority of the members of the bench in a decision in which some of them disagree.

Malfeasance—Commission of an unlawful act.

Mandamus—A writ, issued from a superior court to an inferior court, corporation, or officer, which commands the performance of a legally required public act.

Misfeasance—Improper performance of a lawful act.

Mitigation—The reduction in a fine, penalty, sentence, or damages initially assessed or decreed against a defendant.

Moot case—A case in which the factual controversy no longer exists.

Nolens Jolens—With or without consent.

Nonfeasance—Omission to perform a required duty.

Ordinance—The term applied to a municipal corporations' legislative enactments. An ordinance should be distinguished from a statute.

Petitioner—One who initiates a proceeding and requests some relief be granted on his behalf.

Plaintiff—One who initiated a lawsuit; the party bringing suit.

Plenary—Full, conclusive.

Police power—Legislative prerogative to enact laws for the comfort, health, and prosperity of the state and people.

Precedent—A decision considered as furnishing an example or authority for an identical or similar case afterward arising on a similar question of law.

Prima facie—On its face, evidence supporting a conclusion unless it is rebutted.

Quantum Meruit—An implication that the defendant had promised to pay plaintiff as much as he reasonably deserved for his services.

Referendum—The practice of referring to the voters measures passed by the legislative body for their approval or rejection.

Remand—Send back a case to the court from which it was appealed for further action by the lower court. Ordinarily this return is accompanied with instructions by the superior court as to what further proceedings should be undertaken by the inferior court.

Respondent—Party against whom a legal action is brought, the appellee in a case appealed.

Respondent superior—Responsibility of a master for the acts of his servant.

Restrain—To prohibit from action.

Slander—The malicious deformation of a person in his reputation, profession, or business, by words.

Sovereign Immunity—The freedom of a governmental body from suit without its permission. Sometimes referred to as "governmental immunity."

Statute of Limitations—A statute that sets forth the time period within which litigation may be commenced in a particular cause of action.

Stare decicis—Principle that when a court has made a declaration of a legal principle it is the law until changed by competent authority.

Tort—A private or civil wrong (other than a breach of trust or contract) for which the law requires compensation. Ordinarily, the compensation granted is for injury, either willful or negligent, caused to one's person, property, or reputation.

Ultra Vires—Acts beyond the scope of authority. Outside the legal power of an individual or body.

Vested—The right to or enjoyment of absolute ownership in all or part of real or personal property.

Waiver—To renounce or abandon a right; an intentional or uncoerced release of a known right.

INDEX OF CASES

A

Abramovich v. Board of Education of Cent.
Sch. Dist., 75.
Ahern v. Board of Education, 150.
Alexander v. Alabama State Tenure
Comm., 75.
Alvin Independent School District v.
Cooper, 121, 123
Alyeska Pipeline Co. v. Wildness Society,
58
Anderson Federation of Teachers v.
Schools, City of Anderson, 147
Applebaum v. Wueff, 52
Aquirre v. Tohoka Independent School
District, 106

B

Baker v. Downey Board of Education, 110
Ballard v. Polly, 95
Beeson v. Kiowa City School District, 130
Bell v. Bd. of Educ., 10
Bertrot v. School Dist., No. 1., 25
Black v. Cothren, 107
Blanchet v. Vermillion School Board, 141
Board of Educ. v. Goodpaster, 10
Board of Education v. Marting, 15
Board of Education v. McHenry, 79
Board of Education for Montgomery Co.
v. Messer, 67
Board of Educ. v. Rogers, 10
Board of Education v. Swan, 57
Board of School Dir. of the Centennial
Sch. Dist. v. Sect. of Educ., 71
Boyce v. Board of Educ. of City of Royal
Oak, 73
Braesch v. DePasquale, 131
Braxton v. Board of Public Instruction of
Duval County, 150
Breen v. Kahl, 120
Brown v. Bathke, 54

Burnaman v. Bay City Independent School
District, 75
Burnside v. Byars, 24, 106, 107
Burton v. Cascade School District, Union
High School, 58

C

Calvin v. Rupp, 31
Cantwill v. Connecticut, 23
Cash v. Hock, 107
Chilton v. Cook County School Dist., 94
Clary v. Alexander County Board of Educa-
tion, 97
Collins v. Wolfson, 31
Commonwealth v. Dixon, 114
Conrad v. Goolsby, 142
Connecticut General Statute, 103
Conte v. School Community of Methuen,
66
Cook v. Hudson, 149
Cooper v. Aaron, 5
Corley v. Daunhauer, 120
Crossen v. Fatsi, 107

D

Decanio v. Sch. Committee of Boston, 52,
53
De Old v. Board of Educ. of the Borough
of Verona, 72
Diana v. State Board of Education, 162
Dick v. Board of Education, 79
Dixon v. Alabama State Board of Educa-
tion, 104
Dotter v. Wilson, 26

E

East Hartford Educ. Assoc. v. Board of
Educ. of Town of East Hartford, 24

Elisofon v. Board of Educ. of New York City, 44

ERB v. Iowa State Board of Public Instruction, 54

Everson v. Board of Education, 23

F

Farrel v. Board of Education, 57

Ferguson v. Thomas, 33

Fischler v. Askew, 73

Fitzgerald v. Montgomery County Board of Education, 95

Fitzgibbon v. Board of Educ. of the Twp. of Jefferson, 71

Foster v. Cobb County Board of Education, 94

Fox v. Board of Educ. of the Watchung Hills Reg. High Sch. Dist., 72

Fred C., 117

Freeman v. Flake, 99

Finot v. Pasadena City Board of Education, 142

G

Gault, In re, 104

Gervasio, In re Chris A., 74

Gish v. Board of Educ. of Borough of Paramus, 26

Glover v. Daniel, 55

Goldin v. Board of Education, 144, 145

Gonzales v. McEuen, 130

Goss v. Lopez, 99; 130

Gotkin v. Miller, 31

Graber v. Kniola, 112

Graham v. Knutzen, 99

Gregory v. Small, 57

Guadalupe Organization v. Temple Elementary School District No. 3, 162

Guthrie v. Board of Education of Jefferson County, 52

H

Hillman v. Elliott, 130

Head v. Special School District No. 1, 148

Hobson v. Bailey, 110

Horosko v. School Dist. of Mt. Pleasant, 52; 53

Hortonville Joint School District v. Hortonville Education Association, 150

Hostrop v. Board of Junior College District 515, 31

Hurtado v. California, 29

I

Irizarry v. Anker, 74

J

Jennes v. School District No. 31, 64

Joint Anti-Fascist Committee v. McGrath, 29

Johnson v. Board of Education, 79

Johnson v. Joint School District No. 60, 112

Johnson v. U.S. District Joint School Board, 56

Jordon v. School District of Erie, Ca., 99

Juul v. School District of Manitowoc, 79

K

Kaprelilan v. Texan Women's University, 31

Karp v. Becker, 107

Keefe v. Geanakos, 139

Keyishian v. Board of Regents, 135

Knight v. State Board of Education, 104

Konigsberg v. State Bar of Calif., 28

Kozer, 17 Educ. Dept. Rep., N.Y. Comm'r, 130

L

Lake Michigan College Federation of Teachers v. Lake Michigan Community College, 147

Lanza v. Wagner, 15

Large v. Board of Educ. of the Borough of Roseland, 74

Larry P. v. Riles, 163
Lawson v. Board of Education of Vestal, 148
Leddy v. Board of Education, 57
Leland v. School District No. 28, 64
Levitt v. Board of Educ. of the City of Newark, 72
Lipp v. Board of Educ. of City of Chicago, 30
Long v. Zopp, 120
Lovitt v. Concord School District, 96
Ludwig v. Board of Education, 15

M

Marlar v. Bell, 114, 115
Marsh v. Birmingham Bd. of Educ., 73
Massie v. Henry, 119
Maxwell v. Santa Fe Public Schools, 94
McAuliff v. Mayor of New Bedford, Mass, 138
McLaughlin v. Machias Sch. Committee, 75
McLellan v. Board of St. Louis Public Schools, 57
Mercer v. State, 113
Meyer v. Board of Educ. Affton Sch. Dist., 73
Meyer v. Board of Education, 78
Michael F. Secula, Dec. of N.J. Comm'r of Educ, 71
Miller v. Gillis, 112
Mills v. Board of Education of the District of Columbia, 155, 157
Minnesota General Statute, 103
Mormon v. Board of Education, 15
Morris v. Board of Education of Caurel School District, 57
Morrison v. Hamilton County Board of Education, 150, 141
Morse v. Wozniak, 44

N

Nelson v. State, 116
New Jersey v. Brown, 147
New York Times Co. v. Sullivan, 137
Nicholas v. Echert
North Dakota v. Heath, 151

Norwalk Teacher's Association v. Board of Education of City of Norwald, 146

O

O'Dell v. School District of Independence, 97
Olff v. East Side Union High School District, 120
Ordway v. Hargraves, 122
O.R.S., 68

P

Parrish v. Moss, 151
Pennsylvania Association for Retarded Children v. Commonwealth of Pennsylvania, 155, 157
Perkins v. Inhabitants of Town Standish, 64
Perry v. Granada Mun. Sep. School District, 123
Perry v. Grenada, 122
Pettit v. State Board of Education, 152
Phillippe v. Clinton-Prairie School Corp., 145
Pickering v. Board of Educ., 25, 136, 137
Potts v. Wright, 114

R

Ramsey v. Hopkins, 142
Richards v. Thurston, 119
Robinson v. Sacremento City Unified School District, 111
Rost v. Horky, 25

S

Sarac v. Board of Education (State), 70
Sarac v. State Board of Educ., 53
Sarle v. School District No. 27, 57
School Directors of District No. 1 v. Birch, 55
School District of Dennison Township v. Padden, 57
School District No. 1 v. Parker, 55

School District No. 39 v. Shelton, 64

Shankle v. Board of Educ. of Ontario Local School, 75

Shannon v. Addison Trail High School District, 80

Shull v. Columbus Mun. Sep. School District, 123

Slochower v. Board of Educ., 28

Smith v. Board of Education, 98, 111

Smith v. School District No. 57, 64

Snell v. Brothers, 43

State ex rel. Barney v. Hawkins, 21

State v. Board of Education of Fairfield, 55

State ex. rel. Glover J. Holbrook, 139

State ex rel. Halloway v. Sheats, 21

State ex rel. Idle v. Chamberlain, 121

State ex rel. Kenny v. Jones, 64

State v. Jefferson Parish School Board, 140

State v. Stein, 117

State v. Ward, 113

State v. Young, 113

Stein v. Highland Park Independent School District, 78

Stevenson v. Wheller City Board of Education, 98

Stevenson v. Wheeler County Board of Education, 120

Stone v. Fritts, 68, 67

Strickland v. Berger, 66

Stull v. School Board, 120

Sullivan v. Meade City Independent School District, 144

Sullivan v. Meade Independent School District No. 101, 54

Swain, 17 Educ. Dept. Rep., N.Y. Comm'r Dec. No. 9674, 131

Sweezy v. New Hampshire, 135

Swilley v. Alexander, 138

T

Thompson v. Wake City Board of Education, 54

Tichon v. Harder, 31

Tinker, 109

Tinker v. Des Moines Independent Community School Dist., 23, 104

Turano v. Board of Educ. of Island Trees, 30

U

Underwood v. Board of County School Commissioners, 57

W

Wallace v. Ford, 112

Wassow v. Trowbridge, 104

Westley v. Rossi, 107, 120

Whitacre v. Board of Education, 96

Whitfield v. East Baton Rouge Parish School Board, 78

Wieman v. Updegraff, 27

Wilder v. Board of Education, 15

William Simpson, Dec. of N.J. Comm'r of Educ, 74

Williams v. Board of Educ. of the Twp. of Teaneck, 72

Wilson v. Kroll, 94

Wood v. Strickland, 114

Wright v. Board of Education of St. Louis, 112

Wright v. Consolidated School District, 78

Z

Zeluck v. Board of Education of New Rochelle, 148

SUBJECT INDEX

A

Academic freedom. 134, 139, 150

B

Boards of education
  Composition, 19
  Meetings, 19
  Minutes, 19
  Responsibilities, 20

C

Certification, 67
  Revocation, 68
Chief State Officer, 13
Constitutions, 6
  Statutory construction, 8
Contract of employment
  Abandonment, 66
  Compendium of cases, 71
  Definition, 60
  Dismissal procedures, 65
  elements, 62
  Impairment, 34
  Ratification, 62
  Rights and responsibilities, 64
  Resignation, 66
  Termination, 67, 146
  Types, 61
  Ultra vires, 63
  Void, 63
  Voidable, 63
Control of Pupils
  Conduct, 87
  Errands, 91
  Field trips, 91
  Medical treatment, 91
  Safety patrols, 90
  Tort liability, 92

Transportation, 91
Corporal Punishment
  Guidelines, 88
Courts and Due Process
  Court intervention, 99
  Definition of due process, 103
  Philosophies of Supreme Court, 100
  Students' rights under, 100

D

Dismissal of Teachers
  Cause, 50
  Failure to observe regulations, 56
  Immorality, 53
  Inadequate supervision, 89
  Incompetency, 51
  Insubordination, 55
  Justification, 44
  Neglect of duty, 55
  Unfitness, 54
  Unprofessional conduct, 52
  Remedies, 57
Due Process
  Cases, 129
  Definition, 123
  Federal provisions, 34
  Fifth Amendment, 34
  Fourteenth Amendment, 34
  General welfare clause, 33
  Liberty interest, 30
  Procedural, 29
  Property interest, 30
  Requirements, 124
  Substantive, 29
  Supreme Court Jurisdiction, 34
  Tenth Amendment, 34

F

Federal Role in Education, 3

L

Legal Status of the Local Board, 14
   Tort liability, 78
   Significant responsibilities, 16

M

Management and Control of Public Education, 4

P

Police-School Cooperation, 117
Policy Making
   Content, 17
   Definition, 17
   Value, 17

R

Rights for the Handicapped
   Access rights, 165
   Amendment of records, 165
   Child status, 161
   Civil action, 176
   Continuum of placement, 159
   Definition of handicapped, 168
   Due process procedures, 159, 157
   Hearing, 175
   Historical perspective, 154
   Independent evaluation, 160
   Individual education program, 171
   Individualized instruction, 170
   Initial placement, 172
   Least restrictive alternatives, 158
   Mainstreaming, 170
   Major purpose P.L. 94-142, 167
   Parents access to records, 164
   Parents appeal procedure, 176
   Parental rights, 174
   Physical education exclusion, 169
   Physical education defined, 168
   Protection in evaluation, 173, 162
   P.L. 94-142 defined, 156
   Related services, 168
   Special education, 168
   Vocational education, 169

Teachers' in-service, 177

S

Source of School Law, 5
   Constitutions, 6
   State statutes, 7
   Judicial opinions, 8
State Board of Education
   Duties, 12
   Legal authority, 10
   Recommendations, 11
   Size, 11
State Government and Education, 9
State Statutes, 7
Student Rights and Due Process
   Administrative guidelines, 118
   Dress codes, 112
   Due process, 103
Due process cases, 104-108
   First Amendment rights, 109
   Freedom of assembly, 111
   Hair codes, 119
   Married students, 121
   Searches by school officials, 115
   Search of lockers, 116
   Search and seizure, 113
   Tinker as precedent, 108

T

Teachers Civil Rights and Responsibilities
   Academic freedom, 134, 139, 150
   Certification and appointment, 21
   Conduct, 3
   Dress and appearance, 141
   False statements, 137
   Fifth Amendment, 26
   Fines, 147
   Freedom of association, 26, 143, 149
   Free speech, 25, 137
   Fourteenth Amendment, 29
   Legal status, 20
   Loyalty oaths, 27
   Pleading the Fifth, 28
   Refusing assignments, 151
   Responsibilities, 132
   Restraining order, 147
   Rights outside the classrooms, 145

Strikes, 145, 150
Tenure
  Abrogation, 141
  Default, acquiescence, estoppel, 43
  Defense, 40
  Definition, 37
  Development, 36
  Growth, 38
  Probationary status, 42
  Purpose, 36
  Teachers rights under, 139
  Type laws, 46

Tort
  Defamation, 86
  Defense, 77
  Definition, 76
  Degrees, 81
  Libel, 86
  Negligence, 80
  Redress, 81
  Slander, 85
  Waivers, 90
  Case summaries, 93-97

NC